Connecting *the* Pieces
The Discovery of Early-Onset Bipolar Disorder

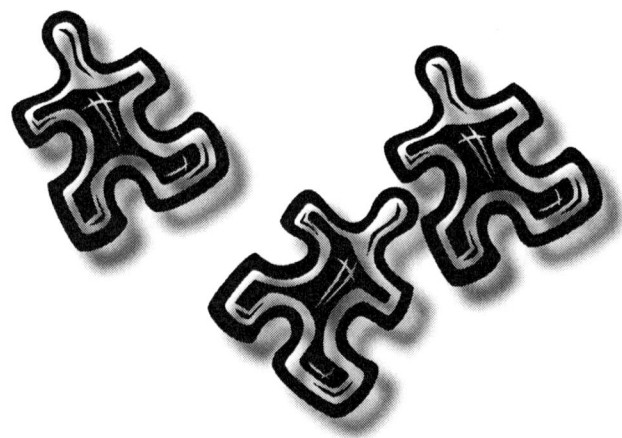

Diane Kratt (mother)
and Ethan Martinez (son)

Order this book online at www.trafford.com/07-0952
or email orders@trafford.com

Most Trafford titles are also available at major online book retailers.

Note for Librarians: A cataloguing record for this book is available from Library
and Archives Canada at www.collectionscanada.ca/amicus/index-e.html

Printed in Victoria, BC, Canada.

ISBN: 978-1-4251-2773-2

Cover Design by Levi at Kwik Kopy

Photograph by Cheryl's Kids Photography

*We at Trafford believe that it is the responsibility of us all, as both individuals
and corporations, to make choices that are environmentally and socially sound.
You, in turn, are supporting this responsible conduct each time you purchase a
Trafford book, or make use of our publishing services. To find out how you are
helping, please visit www.trafford.com/responsiblepublishing.html*

*Our mission is to efficiently provide the world's finest, most comprehensive
book publishing service, enabling every author to experience success.
To find out how to publish your book, your way, and have it available
worldwide, visit us online at www.trafford.com/10510*

www.trafford.com

North America & international
toll-free: 1 888 232 4444 (USA & Canada)
phone: 250 383 6864 ♦ fax: 250 383 6804
email: info@trafford.com

The United Kingdom & Europe
phone: +44 (0)1865 722 113 ♦ local rate: 0845 230 9601
facsimile: +44 (0)1865 722 868 ♦ email: info.uk@trafford.com

10 9 8 7 6 5 4 3 2

Dedicated to all those whose lives have been affected by bipolar disorder

In the middle of difficulty lies opportunity.

-Albert Einstein

Prologue...

Life is in a constant state of change. I knew that, but yet I never expected my life to contain elements in which I had no control over. I assumed that life would change according to my plan. It has taken a situation far more complex and serious than I ever imagined for me to realize that I need to accept the things I cannot change, or that are changing in spite of my best efforts to stop them. I still believe that I have influence over people and situations and I also believe that I do control some aspects of my life, but not all and not other people. As you can imagine, learning a lesson such as this, one usually has to learn the hard way. It was no different for me.

As an educator, I had worked with many students and their parents. Students came to school with varying ability levels and life experiences. There were always students who were well disciplined, respectful, dependable, and enjoyable to have in class. However, there were also students who seemed rebellious, rude, lazy, and challenging to have in class. I firmly believed, and said it countless times, that the students and their behavior were a direct result of the way they were parented and raised. I was of the mind set that a child's environment was the primary way a child received information about what was and was not appropriate behavior. This belief was comforting to me. That meant that I had all the control and through the use of behavior modification techniques, I could maintain the control. Whatever kind of child I wanted, I could produce according to the environment he or she would be exposed to. I felt I had all of the answers. I was 27 years old and had been working with children for the past nine years! I actually had folders full of self —esteem information, good parenting techniques, and child psychology pamphlets. I was completely ready to be a parent and I felt confident that the child I would raise would behave just the way I planned.

In reality, raising my son has been a struggle right from the beginning and that is the story that we are sharing. One reason for putting it in writing is because I actually want a record of all the steps we have taken and the frustration we have experienced on and off for the past twelve years. The other reason is because it made for a great Language Arts project for my twelve year old son whom I am currently home schooling. My son's SPECT scan showed no signs of ADHD, but instead it did show patterns of Traumatic Brain Injury, cyclic mood disorder, anxiety disorder, and rigid cognitive inflexibility disorder. Our therapist said that he was the most frustrated child for his age that she had ever worked with. Obviously, if I could have changed all of this, I would have. What I could change, I did.

Prologue...

My name is Ethan and I am twelve years old. I am being home schooled for a couple more months. Then, I am going back to my old school. The book that I am writing is part of my language arts class. I don't like to write but I thought I should do something nice for my mom, so I am.

I am being home schooled because I am trying to find the right medicine that will make me happy and appreciative. If I were at school I would probably be getting into trouble. I really hated school the past couple of years because of the homework. It was really hard. Hopefully, I can find the right medicine soon.

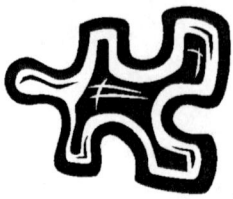

Preparations...

If I knew then what I know now, I would have made much better use of the lessons I learned along the way. I find it amazing how I can look back through the years and see where God was providing me with opportunities to learn and think about essential conditions in other people's lives that I would later be faced with myself. Just the fact that I was interested in working with children from a young age helped to pave the way for my future, but there were a lot more specific things than that.

As a senior in high school I was given the opportunity to be an intern. It was the first year for this program and up until then, there was nothing offered during the high school years that constituted the gifted program in our school district. So, it was exciting to be part of this new program and I still look back fondly on that experience. I interned at our local mental health service agency. It is so hard to believe how perfect that placement was for me. I helped two women teach parenting classes, worked in a daycare for children with birth defects, and I also worked a couple of days a week at a school, then called Children's Personal Development Center (CPDC). This was a therapeutic school for children who were labeled severely emotionally disturbed. There were counselors as well as academic teachers who worked daily with these children. I loved it there and felt badly for the children who had these struggles. That experience was the first glimpse of special needs children that I had.

My original major in college was social sciences. I wanted to be a child psychologist. I definitely had an interest in that area, especially after my internship in high school, but I wasn't sure how to go about being a psychologist. During college, I was hired by the school district as a teacher's assistant and ended up working in the special education department at an elementary school. The school's population was comprised largely of low socio-economic students and had a history of low performing students. I wasn't working there long before I decided to change my major to education. It was something that I loved and understood while at the same time gave me the opportunity to use my interests in the child psychology field as well.

I graduated from college in December of 1989 with a B.S. degree in Elementary Education and have since earned a Master's degree in school age child development. I began teaching for the county's school district immediately. During my time in that system I continued to teach with regards to the individual and with an understanding of differences. Along with regular education, I taught split grade classes, special education inclusion models, and gifted resource classes.

Later, while teaching in another public elementary school, I can remember feeling so drawn to another teacher's personal plight with her own son. This was a woman who was an excellent teacher and always had a positive attitude. It clearly bothered me when she shared with me that her then middle school age son was struggling with mental illness. She was searching for answers and treatment options. Her life had just taken a devastating turn and my heart went out to her. I felt that it hit me like a ton of bricks, even though I didn't know her son. I can remember thinking how terrible that must be for her and how was she going to make it through something like that. Her story stuck with me over the years, but never once did I think I might be able to identify with it. Since writing this, I contacted her and together we shared some common stories and struggles. It was great to reconnect and for me to tell her how much her story had stayed with me.

At the time of her struggles, I was having struggles of my own. Even though I was happy that I had recently given birth to my son, my marriage was not working too well. We weren't married long when I knew that I could not live the way he did. It was hard emotionally and financially for us. I ended up leaving the public school system and teaching at a parochial school. I still believe God led me to this school, but at the time I thought it was really about finances and helping me through my difficult divorce situation. I now believe there were more personal reasons as well.

While at the parochial school, I was given the opportunity to develop and lead a school wide resource program. The intention was to help meet the students' individual needs. I worked with students who needed more enrichment educational programs and those who were struggling to learn the basics. I learned a lot from those students and their families. I read many psychological evaluation reports and doctor recommendations. I also became very familiar with Dr. Mel Levine and his work with brain based learning differences. I began to dabble with brain research myself. There was so much to learn about the cause of each child's struggling. There were so many possibilities and each symptom was a piece to a larger puzzle. Again, I was unaware of how these struggles might foreshadow my own son's struggles.

It was during this time as a resource teacher that I began to look at my son's issues more, but still not seeing them for what they were. I offered no remedial help or accommodations to my own son. I expected him to toe the line and in 5th grade when all hell broke loose, I finally realized that I had better take a closer look at our own life. At that time I had never put the pieces of my own life together in order to make sense. To me, I was amiss chaos with no clear understanding of what was happening. It was as I started to place the pieces together that I could look back and see where all the pieces in my own life made more sense in helping me with what I was dealing with now. I also started to get a clearer picture of my son's situation, but I felt something was still missing. I couldn't make complete sense of Ethan's behavior. I found those missing pieces through prayer, diligence, and a TV show.

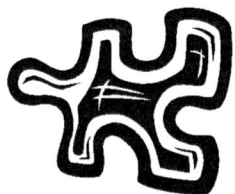

Back to the Beginning...

Child birth was no picnic for us; however, I do not believe at this time that anything that happened during child birth affected our future situation. My epidural did not work properly and the baby had the umbilical cord around his neck, but on June 4, 1994 Ethan Cole Martinez was born. He was healthy and weighed 6lbs 2oz. Both his father and I were excited to finally meet the child whom we already loved.

After his difficult birth, I just figured everything had to get easier. I was wrong. The next problem we encountered was his inability to keep formula down. He started projectile vomiting, which was not amusing. Before we left the hospital, we had started him on soy formula. That seemed to be a better fit for him. After an extended day in the hospital for my benefit, we were able to take him home. I just knew that things were going to be better at home and that having a child was going to be a wonderful experience.

There were things about Ethan that stood out immediately. Some of them were physical traits, like the fact that he has his father's ear lobes, but others had more to do with his mannerisms and personality. I had always assumed that a person's personality developed throughout his/her life, but I know now that there are certain traits recognizable right from the start. I can't tell you how many times someone described him as being so "alert" for such a young baby.

He was only a few days old the first time someone made that comment. I have to admit, my first thought was that it had to do with his intelligence and I can remember feeling proud. He is still very alert and has great observations, only now I attribute the alertness to the overactive brain he seems to have been born with.

I wasn't wrong about his intelligence though. Ethan met all of the baby milestones early and clearly was an abled learner right from the beginning. Language skills were easy for him to master. He has always had a lot to say and clearly understood the things that were asked of him. I found his learning to be fascinating and enjoyed watching how he learned new concepts and grew intellectually each week. Many times I was surprised at his extensive vocabulary or his determination to accomplish a task.

He has always been a physically active child too. He took his first steps at nine and a half months and he has been on the go since. Not only is he active, he also has great physical coordination which has enabled him to perform many perilous feats. He insisted on climbing and crawling out of his crib by a year old, so we made his crib into a toddler bed for him. Keeping him in that bed was a lot harder, but it was safer because it was lower to the ground.

Getting him to sleep was a difficult task that continues to be a problem for him. I can remember placing him in his swing for what seemed like hours before he would finally doze off. If not the swing, then it was one of us rocking him to sleep. We tried different musical tapes, books, and even our own singing to help him fall asleep. We did try to leave him in his crib to put himself to sleep like different experts recommended, however, Ethan never seemed to settle down. It seemed like he would literally cry for days instead of falling asleep. We tried this technique for days at a time with no sign of improvement. It then felt as if it bordered on abuse, so we gave up that idea and went back to the swing or rocking chair.

Ethan was always busy and easily drew everyone's attention. People generally found him cute and fun to be around. Although it was tiring to look after him, people usually didn't mind. However, he was also stubborn and demanding at times. During these times, it was hard to figure out what had happened and what it was going to take to get him to calm down. No matter which mood he was in at the time, his care takers always had to work for their money.

There were a few short months in which we took Ethan to the hospital day care center while we were at work. My mother worked there and Ethan only had to be there about 4 or 5 hours each day. I can remember the infant room teacher telling me that Ethan was quite a handful at 4 months old. She noticed that he really did not like to have his diaper changed or be restrained in any way. She laughed while she was telling me and I was a new, proud mom so I didn't think much of any of it. There was nothing wrong with the day care center or our experience, but we had the opportunity for Ethan to stay with a friend who had just had a daughter and was going to stay home with her. Even though her house was several miles out of the way, we jumped at the opportunity of Ethan being able to have a relaxed, home environment. Jill was a teacher and had an easy going, calm personality. I felt that he would thrive in that environment. He stayed with Jill for most of the first 2 and half years of his life. Jill would write me little notes and always had stories to tell me about his day. She said that he and her daughter, Donna, were complete opposites. Jill also felt that Ethan had very boyish interests, was active, aggressive, stubborn, intelligent, and enjoyable all at the same time. As he got older she was concerned with the fact that even though he learned easily, he didn't seem to learn from the negative consequences of his behaviors. It was frustrating to constantly redirect or correct him for the same behaviors time after time again. I totally could relate to that.

I have a vivid memory from when Ethan was a toddler. I was sitting on my bed crying because I was so tired of him doing the same things over and over again. I knew he was smart, but I couldn't understand why he hadn't learned. I was trying time out, as was suggested by our pediatrician, and saying no very sternly. I even resorted to spanking his hand. But, day after day he would continue to do the same little things he was not supposed to do. When I corrected him, he would throw fits of anger for awhile but go back and do the same things again. I felt frustrated and totally incompetent as a mother. I called my neighbor friend, who had a toddler at home too, and we spoke about it. She tried to comfort me and we prayed together, but the problem never did go away.

When Ethan was two and a half years old his sitter, Jill, was expecting a new baby and decided that she could not continue to keep Ethan any longer. As I went around looking for preschools, I realized right away that there were not too many I would consider for us. I also realized the expense of preschool and how wonderful Jill's fee had been. I ended up liking a parochial school in our community the best. The children needed to be screened and they needed to be 3 years old to attend. I went ahead and applied for St. Matthew Lutheran School, but they could not take him until the fall (if they even had room for him then). So, I placed him in Best Friends Preschool when he was two and a half while we waited for acceptance at St. Matthew in the fall. I found that I really loved Best Friends because of their nurturing environment and exceptional staff. He ended up staying there for six months. In that time his teacher had a few conversations with me about his behavior when he didn't get things his way. I am sure it was common for two year olds to behave that way at times, but both his teacher and I realized that his temper and stubbornness was a bit excessive. Even at that time, he was having difficulty with his peers as well. We also noticed a mean streak in him that went against his loving nature. It has continued to exist and causes us concern at times. Being mean just isn't normal and was a red flag for me. Everyone always comments on the "terrible twos", so most people thought everything was typical at that age. Unfortunately, he never outgrew that stage. At times, his behavior continues to be very similar to what a two year old is like.

One of the things that separated his behavior from that of the average child his age was that his fits of rage after being told no would be more extreme and last longer than a typical temper tantrum. They were also more frequent and no matter how much I stuck to my guns and didn't give in, this behavior did not stop. He continued to melt down over and over again even if he never received what he wanted in the first place.

It was also around this time that Ethan's father and I separated. Because it was a difficult time in general, it was easy to blame the stress of the situation for all the problems that existed. Even though Joey, his father, had many positive traits, he seemed to struggle with himself on an increasing basis. He would go from being extremely helpful and kind to angry and resentful in the course of a few weeks. He was in a recovery program for alcoholism but seemed to fall off the wagon in a regular pattern. At the time, I never saw a correlation between Joey's struggles and Ethan's issues. I just knew that I couldn't survive if I stayed in that situation with him. Life was like walking on egg shells and a disaster ready to happen at any moment. I wanted to save myself and to be able to maintain a calm, stable lifestyle for Ethan. We divorced just before Ethan turned four years old after being separated over a year and watching Joey's condition worsen instead of get better like I had hoped.

It was during this whole time of turmoil that I became increasingly involved in the church and with friends from the church. We attended The Vineyard along with our neighbors. We also had a small group that met on a weekly basis and I often took classes on Wednesday nights at a local Baptist church. These relationships helped me to see things through and to not lose sight of what really mattered. Even through all of my marital and financial issues, I believe that I spent more time praying for and about Ethan. I was finding it difficult to parent him and to accept traits in him I was uncomfortable with. I also felt that I was having little to no influence over his actions. I prayed so hard to be the best parent for him and for guidance as to what I should do.

That summer, I got a call from St. Matthew Lutheran School asking if I could come in and speak with the administration. It seemed that a teacher I worked with in the past was now teaching fifth grade at St. Matthew. She saw me there in the spring with Ethan and knew he was on their waiting list, so she had put my name in for a possible teaching position that had recently opened as her 5th grade teaching partner. When I went in to speak with them, they not only offered me a job, but said that Ethan could attend there and his tuition would be free. I felt that this was an answer to my prayers for finances as well as a Christian direction for our lives. So, in the fall of 1997 both of us became part of the St. Matthew family.

Mrs. Moore was Ethan's first teacher at St. Matthew in the three year old class. He was adorable at that age. He was enjoyable to have conversations with and a very quick learner. He loved all the wonderful things they were learning in her class and regularly shared them with me. In the four year old class, his friendships started to blossom. There were a group of boys who just had a great time in Mrs. Conner's pre-k 4 class. He began to get invited to birthday parties and started to build friendships that would last for years to come. Mrs. Conner noticed that positive rewards and words worked best for Ethan, and thus began our use of countless sticker charts at home.

Unfortunately, the preschool years were also the time when I first started to become aware of new concerns and situations with him. Ethan remained temperamental and was still often upset if things did not go the way in which he expected them to go. But I also noticed that he had difficulty joining in with others (especially in a positive way). He did not want to participate in activities at school even though he seemed to love doing them at home with me. He would become very stubborn when it was insisted that he contribute. This also happened with sports. Because he was so coordinated and active, it seemed appropriate to allow him to get involved in some sports at the local YMCA geared for preschool age children. He loved whatever it was at home, but would refuse to join in when we got there. I am embarrassed to say that I became very frustrated with him refusing to participate and the fact that I was paying money for him to just sit with me. The way I mishandled his behavior is one of my regrets. I wish I could have seen it for the anxiety disorder that it was and handled it much differently than I did. He was also very bossy around other children and sometimes did mean things to them. Again, I was embarrassed and frustrated so the root of the problem was not sought, just punishment.

The anxiety he had showed up as separation anxiety as well. He would throw huge fits about leaving me whether it was at school or at home. He wanted to be with me as much as possible. An ironic side to it though is that when we were together around other people his behavior was even worse than when I was there. I had to stop teaching his Sunday school class because his behavior was so bad while I was teaching. I was also asked to not volunteer in his preschool classes for the same reason. I even had to avoid seeing him in the halls of our school because of the disruption it would usually cause. At home, we did almost everything together. We spent a lot of time outside in our yard, taking walks, and bike rides because his behavior was much better while busy and doing things he liked. He had learned to ride his bike at three years old (without training wheels), so it became a hard task to keep him contained in our yard. If we rode bikes together, it seemed to be easier and more fun. During these years, our bond grew pretty strong although I constantly tried to remain the parent and was careful not to allow our roles to equalize. He already tended to be bossy and wanted to control things, so I worked at trying to remain the one in charge as the parent in our relationship. I determined what we were going to have for dinner or what roads we were taking to reach our destination, even though things like this often resulted in a fit for Ethan. It amazes me that all of my efforts seemed to have been in vain. It is hard to tell that he has not been allowed to run the show or call the shots by observing his behavior today.

Playing with him was usually no fun for me or for other children. If we were playing a board game, he had to win or else he would throw a huge fit. If we were playing an imaginary game with trucks or something, he had to tell me what to say and where to go. If I would stray from his exact instructions, we would have a problem on our hands. Now don't just think I followed along happily. I tried explaining to him how to play, I tried expressing how it made me feel, I tried not playing and role playing, I tried doing it my own way on purpose. When he had play dates, I tried playing with them to model how to play and to referee the problems (and there were always problems). I was determined to reshape his play behavior, but it has never changed.

Many children of preschool age enjoy videos and TV shows. He wasn't interested in any of it much at all. He would rather be playing and doing instead of just watching. I knew it was good to not have too much TV time, but I have to admit that I would have enjoyed a little quiet time with him being absorbed in a movie or show for awhile. One show that he did watch sometimes was *Mr. Roger's Neighborhood*.

Another thing that came to my attention during his preschool years was how lack of sleep seemed to affect his mood and behavior. He was very active in school and was not able to rest easily and nap as the other children did. Mrs. Moore talked with me about sleep. I assured her that he went to bed at a good time each night and that we had a whole bedtime routine. She suggested we move the bedtime earlier and I did. Not only did he go to sleep right after dinner now, but I stayed in his room and put him to sleep instead of letting him lay there for an hour falling asleep on his own. This was a blessing. He slept longer and seemed better off the next day for it. Since that time, sleep has been an extremely important part of Ethan's life as well as a symptom of his disorder. Unfortunately, I have had to help him fall asleep much of the time for all these years too.

Ethan was easily excited and seemed to have some great loves. He really enjoyed water. When it was hard to keep him satisfied and involved in something, I could always use water. He loved taking baths and I could read a chapter in my book while sitting in the bathroom with him. He also loved buckets of water or a flowing hose so I would work in the yard sometimes while he played. The beach was probably the best place to go with Ethan. He loved the water's edge and the sand. He became fascinated with dolphins and whales at this age and the beach was a great place for him to act out scenes from the movie *Free Willy.* I loved that I didn't have to fight to restrain him all the time. He had more freedom and space at the beach. He had always hated to be restrained in anything like a car seat, stroller, highchair, etc., so this kind of activity was well suited to his personality.

He has also always loved vehicles, especially big ones. I believe bus was one of his first words and he longed to ride a school bus until he finally got his opportunity at age 11. He has watched and studied every semi truck, construction vehicle, and trailer that exists. He has always been excited about driving vehicles. He would drive anything that you possible would allow him to drive. I wonder if his love for it has anything to do with having control over something or possibly the ability to push your physical boundaries. To this day, trucks are absolutely his greatest love.

PIECES TO THE PUZZLE

- Alert

- Quick learner

- Trouble falling asleep

- Didn't like to be restrained

- Easily frustrated

- Wanted things to go his way

- Well-coordinated

- Not responsive to negative consequences

- Trouble entering a group

- Separation anxiety

- Physically active

- Aggressive at times

- Mean streak

- Reached baby milestones early

- Liked predictability and routine

- Temper tantrums

In the Beginning ...

I don't remember very much from when I was under five years old. We do have some videos and photos that I have seen. That was when my dad lived at home with us. I can tell that I was cute and that I got to do a lot of fun things with family and friends. I do remember learning how to ride my bike without training wheels, and mom says that I was only three years old then. She also said that I was less than one year old when I learned to walk and about one when I started to talk.

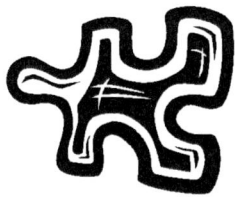

Primary Grades...

In his Kindergarten school year at St. Matthew, with Mrs. Hall, my most vivid memory is of him wearing high socks up to his knees. No one else wore them, but to Ethan, it was the only option. Thankfully, I did not fight it or many other clothing issues. There were a few other memories from kindergarten too. They were learning to print the letters at school and I remember that he always wanted to erase his writing in order to get it perfect. He learned to read and he was so proud of himself. Mrs. Hall discovered that he would hit people when he got mad. This surprised her, but I was already familiar with this method from infancy. I had tried everything I knew to keep him from lashing out, but to no avail. He was accused of whipping a classmate during PE with a jump rope that year, but Ethan claimed he was only trying to capture him. His teacher told me that she could tell he was taught how to behave because he always knew the right answer, but it didn't always work for him. He also didn't want to have to work at figuring things out. He expected to know everything right then. It was especially true with adding numbers. He just wanted them all memorized so there would be no work involved. He is still like that today; he likes things immediately instead of working for it. He had an excellent memory, especially for numbers so it made sense to him. It was the very beginning of his kindergarten year when he explained to me that he didn't like the beginning of school because it took him a little while to get used to new things. Wow! How true that has turned out to be.

I often turn to information to help me deal with a problem, so I started to look for books that could help me be a better parent for him. I read some of James Dobson's books, like *The Strong-willed Child*, and they were good to read. I also read a book called *The Difficult Child* that we had in our school library. I started to feel that maybe Ethan just had a temperament that was more challenging and I would just have to work harder at parenting him. As I look back, I see that my parenting role has been one of a researcher. I have read so many books from before he was even born until now that it would be impossible to recount all of them. I have also watched videos, gone to listen to speakers, sought counsel from many people, tried various behavior programs, and even taken classes. One such class was about the various love languages where I learned that Ethan seemed to favor physical touch and words of affirmation. Most of my efforts proved to be interesting, but not very effective in our real life. Thank goodness I did not give up my researcher role though, because it finally paid off for us down the road.

Ethan began playing soccer during his kindergarten year. His coach was a father of one of his classmates and really tried to encourage Ethan. His athletic ability should have provided him with enough motivation and eagerness to be the team's star player. Unfortunately, his anxiety got the best of him. He played to only half of his ability a good bit of the time. His coach felt that he had low self esteem. I was in shock again. I knew about low self esteem and I worked hard to make sure my child would have great self esteem. I was intentional at doing things to promote positive self esteem where many parents don't even consider it while they are parenting. I couldn't figure out how or why he would have low self esteem. Again, anxiety never entered my mind. Even if it had, I wouldn't have understood it. What could he possibly be afraid of or nervous about? When I look back now, I know the answer. At such an early age, he was already worried about how others perceived him. He didn't want to mess up and he didn't want to be embarrassed. He didn't want others to make fun of him and laugh. How do I know? Because these are the same struggles he has today, only now he is better at verbalizing part of it and I'm better at understanding it. He has continued to play soccer each year, even now. He got used to playing for one association for five consecutive years. Then he played at St. Matthew for two years with kids he had been friends with for along time so he was comfortable again. He is now playing for a new team, with a different coach, on at another field. He is acting very similarly to that time when he first started at age five.

First grade was a big year for us and not just because he lost his first tooth. Thankfully, Ethan was with a teacher whom he loved and she had the patience of a saint. He always felt accepted and loved by Mrs. Warner and I have always appreciated that. We had a big change that year in our life. I married Jim, the man I had been dating for the past two years, and we moved into his house. Adjusting to a new house and a new family caused some stress for Ethan.

I was using various reward/consequence charts to help me be consistent with discipline. I felt that mostly it was keeping Ethan punished the majority of the time. It was awful that he consistently went to bed early, missed dessert, lost privileges, etc. The rewards were never enough to keep him from making the same negative mistakes or choices. Being in a new marriage put pressure on me to be a good mother and have my child behave properly. It was often a bone of contention between Jim and I which only added to an already stressful situation. After a while, I gave up on the various systems and just tried to be a good parent naturally.

There were some major developments though that took place during first grade. One was that I discussed with other adults, and his doctor, the possibility of him having ADD or ADHD. It was really the only thing I could think of and so many children were being diagnosed with it all the time. I personally knew of a boy who was taking medicine for ADHD and I saw how much it benefited him, not to mention all the students I had seen in my class room helped by the medicine. I decided to have him evaluated by a psychologist. I really needed to know if there was a problem with Ethan, or if it was me who had the problem. Dr. Spillburg did not want to talk with us, like therapy. He only wanted to have Ethan tested. I agreed to it, but Dr. Spillburg and I didn't hit it off too well. He seemed upset that I was an informed parent and a professional. He even made comments about my professional vocabulary and told me I didn't need to use that kind of terminology. I think it upset him when I used the word peer when I was referring to how he interacted with his classmates. He was definitely not interested in what I had to say. When the testing came back he said everything was fine. He would not give me any of his test results and I became very frustrated. He suggested play therapy for Ethan and said that both Ethan's and my expectations were too high. When the written report came in, I was irate. So much of the report was wrong that it made all of that evaluation obsolete to me. When I made corrections and sent it back with a letter, he changed some of the problems but not all of them. He gave me very few of the actual test results in the end and I felt totally mistreated by him. I wish I would have filed a complaint because I have spoken to other parents since then who have had similar experiences with him. It is a shame that there are parents still using him and looking to him for answers.

I then took another route. I took Ethan to see one of the pediatricians in the practice that we have always used. Dr. Richmond happily gave me a prescription of Adderall for Ethan to try after discussing what had happened so far and reviewing a checklist that I had filled out from our school. He took it for a few days and it was terrible. He was crying all of the time and was very sad. His whole demeanor was different. Mrs. Warner and I both felt that this was not the answer. I stopped the medication trial prior to the two weeks because I was sure that it was not working correctly. I took it as an answer to my prayers, that Ethan did not have ADHD. So I didn't even want to try other medications for it. I had to wonder if maybe Dr. Spillburg was right and there was nothing wrong. Maybe I did have too high of expectations and I was imagining all of the problems.

One other development was that during the second half of the school year I noticed some tics or obsessions. The worst was that he seemed to pick at his bottom all of the time. I couldn't figure out what was going on. I tried all sort of possibilities, even looking for worms. No treatment made it stop. He played little league T-ball that year and I remember him picking at himself every time he was out in the field. It really wasn't his sport, he only liked to bat; and because it was a "new" activity for him, he had difficulty getting used to it. When the season was done, he said he didn't want to play again. So far, he hasn't. The picking eventually faded away, thank goodness. I believe now that it was stress induced and as he got used to our lifestyle changes, he became more relaxed.

The third development was that I read a great book. I still read through it today and advise others to read it too. It was called *The Explosive Child* by Ross Greene. I learned a lot by reading his book. I had a better understanding of the possibility that behavior and social skills could lag behind just as reading skills could. I felt differently about our situation and also learned to concentrate on the most important issues with Ethan while leaving things that didn't matter as much alone. I still try to implement ideas from this book into our everyday life. I even refer to things as being in basket C, which is directly from his advice.

Mrs. Warner wrote some wonderful comments on Ethan's report cards. It showed different sides of him, the bright, eager, kind child and the side of him where he contradicts his friends, uses negative ways to get attention, and spends a lot of time alone on the play ground. He was a great reader and his academics in general were all in check. She kept stating each quarter that his social skills were lacking and he just needed time and an opportunity to practice them. I understood what she was saying, but it was still frustrating to me because he shouldn't be having problems with social skills. Besides playing T-ball, he was still playing soccer and this year he also joined Cub Scouts as a Tiger. I modeled positive social skills all the time for him, gave him plenty of opportunities to play with friends, and worked on these skills all of the time. What she was seeing is how he acted at home all of the time (only less intense, I'm sure). I have always found it interesting that Ethan's personality really is people oriented. He loves socializing and is generally well liked. However, he always seems to have problems with people after awhile, especially children his own age.

During the summer between first and second grade, I read another good book. It was all about alternative treatments to ADD/ADHD. I looked for a doctor in our area and Ethan began seeing Dr. Altman. She looked for food allergies and found some evidence of slight food allergies in things like milk, eggs, wheat, corn, etc. We also discussed nutrition in general and started Ethan on a much stricter diet. He was given soy milk, protein shakes, flax seed oil, and daily vitamins. He also tried some of the remedies of homeopathic medicine since I could not find serious side effects to them.

We continued this treatment all through his second grade year at school. Mrs. Shuman was his teacher and she is also a good friend of mine. I'm sure he was placed in that class because of her teaching style. She runs a tight ship and is very consistent with discipline. Each student had a car which began each day on the green light. It was moved to yellow or red because of their behavior choices throughout the day. Consequences and rewards were administrated daily. I could always keep track of his behavior based on the color he was on. It seemed like he was on yellow or red quite a bit, at least a lot more often than I would have liked. I think it was a combination of his teacher's style, our alternative treatment regime, and adjustment to our new home life that helped to make this school year one of the easiest he has had. Ethan continued to read a lot and accumulate a large number of Accelerator Reader points. He didn't seem to have any difficulty with academics. He had a good friend in this class which he played with each day. His name is Keith and Ethan was so disappointed when he transferred to another school at the end of 2nd grade. In looking over his report cards, I notice that he had the most trouble in self control and being respectful towards peers. I remember one incident that school year where he killed a caterpillar for no reason and Mrs. Shuman was very upset about it. He lost his recess that day. I also remember that they studied different countries that year and when they studied Mexico, Ethan was excited about that. He asked his Grandma Martinez to make some authentic Mexican food for him to share with his class, which she did.

Ethan got to experience some trauma during the second grade school year. I had taken him to the ice skating rink and he was having a great time. I got off the ice for a few minutes and went to the snack area to warm up again. While I was gone, Ethan fell on the ice and someone stepped on his fingers. They were badly cut and an ambulance was called. I ended up driving him to the emergency room and having his fingers stitched up. We had to visit the pediatric orthopedic office a few different times to get them back to normal. He still has scars today and the nail bed on one of his fingers will never be normal again. This was another opportunity to blame myself and feel guilty again since I had not been right there along side of him when he fell.

He also had some great experiences and made some great memories during this time in his life. Each summer, Jim and I took all three boys on a family vacation during the summer months. We would go to Wisconsin, where Jim's family lives, but would also visit other areas. Twice we spent time in North Carolina where we would mine for gems, swim in the rivers, look for the falls, and go white water rafting. The summer after Ethan finished 2nd grade, we went to Virginia and Washington D.C. before heading to Wisconsin. We visited Williamsburg, Busch Gardens, Norfolk, Arlington, and all the great sites in D.C. Thankfully, we kept journals of our travels so we can look back on our trips and make our memories even more concrete. The memories of the boys on those trips may be what most parents experience. They are filled with both good and bad times for each of them. It was exhausting trying to keep the peace and keep everyone entertained for sure. But it is well worth the work involved to have memories and experiences that last forever.

Even though Ethan is an only child and comes from a divorced family, he has always been supported by family members. There has never been a reason for him to seek out attention like he seems to do. The grandparents would participate in Grandparents' Day at St. Matthew, my siblings have always included him in their events and participated in his, and Joey's family has remained close as well. Joey has not always kept regular scheduled visits or even phone calls, but he has never walked out of his life completely. Anytime Joey was able to spend time with Ethan, I tried to make that time available for him. I encouraged their relationship and have been honest with Ethan about his father's situation. Through my new marriage, Ethan gained a step father and two step brothers. He enjoyed their company and we have tried to do many things together as a family. I guess what I am getting at is, it was not an ideal situation for Ethan, but it was not horrible either. He has been loved by many people and has gotten the attention of everyone who he has come in contact with. Most of the time people really want to spend time with him. He has not lacked for attention, support, or love even though I am sure he would prefer to have a typical nuclear family with siblings and parents who are all healthy and love each other deeply (*Leave it to Beaver* style). Even though others may have felt that Ethan's behaviors and moods were a result of a dysfunctional family environment, I do not feel that this situation caused the social problems he was having or made his temperament the way it was, however, it may have added to an already existing problem.

Pieces to the Puzzle

- Tested the limits
- Tics
- Strong academically
- Athletic
- Well coordinated
- Energetic and active
- Needed time to get used to things
- Afraid of the dark
- Cried easily
- Negative consequences didn't work
- Fears
- Stubborn
- Needed me with him to fall asleep
- Temper tantrums
- Wanted immediate gratification
- Sensitive
- Hard time playing with children his own age
- Attention-seeking behaviors
- Independent and competent
- Separation anxiety
- Intense

Early Elementary School ...

In kindergarten, my favorite activity was to build things out of connecting toys. We put sheets over the toys and played house. I had lots of friends and I liked kindergarten. We learned phonograms and learned how to read. It was my first year playing soccer. My team had yellow shirts and my friend's dad was our coach. I was pretty good and liked playing.

Mrs. Warner was my first grade teacher. She used to talk about all the bad things Suzy Q would do and how we don't want to be like that. I liked Mrs. Warner a lot. I played grapefruit little league. I was on the Giants. I didn't like baseball because it wasn't fun. All I liked was hitting and I couldn't do that very often.

In second grade, I got reminders a lot. Mrs. Shuman was strict and I would get mad because I couldn't do things the way I wanted to do them. She had cars for each of us and we had to move our car if we got too many reminders. I was on yellow and red a lot. She isn't as strict when I'm not in her class. My good friend that year was Keith. We played together at recess every day. I was James Madison in our grade level play. I went to a doctor and she had my blood tested for allergies. I remember that I was allergic to milk, wheat, and eggs (but only a little bit). She was a chiropractor and would crack my back some times with a little metal tool.

I had a bad injury in second grade. I was ice skating with my mom and I fell. Someone stepped on my fingers with their ice skate and cut three fingers. They called an ambulance, but my mom drove me to the hospital instead. I had to get a lot of stitches and had my hand bandaged up. There are still scars on my fingers from the accident.

Intermediate Grades...

I now realize that up until about third grade, I was mostly concerned with how Ethan's difficulties affected me. It was not intentional, nor is it easy to admit, but none-the-less true. I worried about my parenting skills, reputation, leisure time, etc. Ethan seemed to be doing okay. He made good grades in school and was certainly learning a lot. He had the things he needed and spent a great deal of time having fun and playing. He ended up getting things his way a lot of the time because it was so hard dealing with him when he didn't. It seemed his life was fine. Mine, on the other hand was not so fine and that was what concerned me. I prayed continuously for me to learn to accept him as he was, but told myself each day that I could "fix" him if I tried hard enough or was a good enough parent. The contradiction was apparent to others, but I kept trying to fool myself.

Third grade is one of those grades that have a lot of growth and development for children. It is a year of transitioning between being a little kid to an older child. Often, a student either catches up and it evens out at third grade or they continue to separate further. It may be obvious, but Ethan started to separate from his classmates that year. My stance on his situation changed dramatically because of what I witnessed. Nothing was terribly overt, but there were enough small signs to do the trick for me. Ethan's lack of social skills, like being in other students' business, was beginning to sever relationships with his fellow classmates. He also decided that he couldn't read the longer chapter books with smaller print. He still excelled in some academic areas, but there were small signs of future academic difficulty. The worst change in Ethan was the fact that he became unhappy. His self esteem lowered because of his experiences and he knew there was something different about him. He began talking about hating himself and his life. He cried more often. Seeing him miserable made me finally see this as something that he could not control and therefore it was not something I was going to be able to control in him. I felt that I had to do something and I wanted more than anything to make a good decision for him. I kept thinking about the idea that a medication might be the answer that could totally change the way he felt about himself and the way other children saw him. I wanted him to be happy and to be the best he could be.

His teacher, Mrs. King, spoke to me about her thoughts on his behavior. She noticed that he had problems with self control, impulsivity, and social relationships. It looked like ADHD again to both of us. In October of third grade, I took Ethan back to the doctor based on my decision that it must be something he can't help and maybe a medication could help him. We saw Dr. Richmond again, the pediatrician. This time, he prescribed Concerta. It is another stimulant medication used to treat ADD/ADHD disorder. When Ethan started to take the medicine it worked well. Everyone noticed a difference immediately. His teacher reported that stayed in his seat and was not calling out. I noticed that he was much less active and easy to keep up with. Ethan even noticed a difference. I remember him saying to me in the car one day that now he was an artist. He was happy because he could sit still long enough to work on an art picture where as before he would start things and lose interest after just a minute. Ethan liked to take the medicine because he thought it was helping him.

That school year he went on to make some great memories. He won first place in our county for an essay he wrote about going to the Sebring races. He got to go to McDonald's for lunch for being one of the top three in his class at learning the multiplication facts the fastest. Their class trip was a visit to Sea World where he and I had a great day together. Feeding the dolphins was our favorite activity. They learned a lot about sharks that year and Ethan wrote a report on the Lemon Shark. He joined my Odyssey of the Mind team and started to experience team work and creative problem solving skills. Unfortunately, along with all these great times there were also some not so great times. He began to have some anger problems as the year went on. He was still having difficulty with friends and we had to increase his dose of medication towards the end of the year because it didn't seem to be helping as much anymore.

As usual, summer was a welcome change. Ethan has always enjoyed the summers because he has more time to be outside and fewer demands are made on him. It has been great that I have the summers off as well so that we have always spent a lot of time together. Time at the beach/pool continued to be one of our favorite activities. I was hopeful that now that things had calmed down again, Ethan would settle into another school year just fine on the Concerta.

Ethan noticed a difference in his fourth grade teacher right away. He was very happy to be in her class and although he had liked all of his teachers, he said that she was his favorite. Mrs. Macon had a calming nature and was always smiling. Her love of children and teaching really shows through in the class room. She noticed that even though Ethan was often "caught holding the bag", there were others involved as well. He felt that she liked him and understood him. He also didn't feel as much pressure in her class to perform or to be so detailed.

One of his best memories of school is going to Sea Camp in fourth grade. They all went to the Keys for two nights and learned marine biology with their on site instructors. Ethan could not say enough about the trip, the activities, the counselors, and the bus ride. He was in heaven! Honestly, if education could be done in that manner all of the time, we would see huge differences in the children and educational system. No misbehavior was reported to me with that trip and I was thrilled that he had such a good time. I remember that when he got his photos back, there was one of him and his friend, Irwin, with ink all over their faces. They had dissected a squid and used the ink to decorate themselves for a photo. It is priceless.

This was also the first year for band. Ethan had been looking forward to band for several years. He loved music and most instruments since he was little. Playing the drums turned out to be his favorite, so he joined the percussion team for the St. Matthew's band. That class is not as structured as a regular class, so there were times when it was not so easy for him to control himself. All in all, he loved band class, the teacher, and he loved playing the drums. It seemed to be a good fit for him.

He continued to do well in many academic areas. He won another essay contest with a savings bond as a prize. He also was named an honorable mention for the Keep Lee County Beautiful calendar contest for the second year in a row. He was placed in the advanced math class which was very rigorous. His report cards were good all the way through 4th grade.

Ethan seemed to be having trouble with reading that year. It had once been a strong area for him and he used to have a high number of AR points, but not any more. He began to hate reading. He thought the books were too long and boring. Now for someone who loves reading and has promoted it from day one, it was hard for me to take. I thought that there had to be a reason for this situation and I blamed it on ADHD again. I took him to an eye doctor, Dr. Daniel, who checked children for vision and other eye problems. He felt that Ethan's eye movement while reading was the problem. He couldn't track the words efficiently along with other smaller issues. I enrolled him in an eye therapy program for thousands of dollars and a lot of our time. He went twice a week and did all the homework that went along with the program. When he was finished, his tracking did improve up to grade level. I was pleased with that, but disappointed that it did not help him to want to read. I believe now that his over active brain patterns are what makes it hard for him to concentrate and focus while reading. I also believe that it contributed to his tracking difficulty.

As the year progressed, we had some of the usual problems occur again. It seemed that the medicine was not helping as much, so we increased the dose. He seemed to get angry a lot more the second half of the school year. These outbursts were for small things like being told no, having something go a different way than he thought it should, getting upset with other children, etc., much the same as when he was a toddler. While it mostly showed up at home, it was also seen in school at times. In one of our visits with Dr. Richmond, I brought up the possibility of Ethan having bipolar disorder because his father had once been diagnosed with it. The doctor assured me that this was not the case and said that his behavior would be much worse if it were. I had no reason to doubt him at the time and actually had a sense of relief.

Ethan had trouble getting along with some of the other children again. While he was cementing some good friendships with Sam, Irwin, and Lori, he was also isolating himself from other school groups. He would be bossy and not conform. He would feel like kids were picking on him or talking about him and get defensive. His insecurities showed a lot more, but I just couldn't figure out what he could be insecure about. He was a nice looking, smart, athletic boy. He had every reason in the world to be liked and to be happy, but often times he wasn't either.

He had a serious incident towards the end of that school year. While at recess, he had taken a sharp instrument and scratched a parked car through the fence. Destroying someone's property was not a regular past time for him and I was mortified to hear about it. I found out the car was not even someone from our school but instead belonging to a medical worker at the offices next door. I was glad that the principal took care of all the communication, so that I did not have to get involved. I was so embarrassed and just knew that all the kids had gone home and told their parents what he had done. I insisted that he pay for the damages to the car with his own money and was happy when it was all behind us. I wondered why he would have done such a thing and though I still don't know for sure, I think I have a better understanding. He says that one of the girls told him to do it and so he did. Why? Maybe because he is impulsive, maybe because he is so overly worried about other students liking and accepting him, maybe because he wanted to but never thought he should before and maybe because of all or none of those reasons. I don't really know for sure.

Ethan was still part of the Odyssey of the Mind team. We both found his membership difficult, but for different reasons. He had a hard time putting in the work that was needed and trying to get along with everyone. He also has always had a really hard time having me as both a mom and a teacher or coach. He didn't have to be on the team, but a part of him really wanted to be and he didn't want to give it up. He was really good at building things out of PVC pipe and wood. He mostly was a set and prop guy for the team. That year, his team made it all the way to World Finals in Maryland. There they came in third place. It was amazing and the experience was incredible. I was glad that he got to participate and enjoy it, but I knew that it came at a high price for him.

Even though he was about to turn ten years old, he was still having problems falling asleep and getting a good night's rest. He insisted that I come into his room when he went to bed each night. He would be afraid that something bad was going to happen if I wasn't there. He also had a hard time resting and being still enough to fall asleep. If I wasn't in there insisting that he lie still, he would literally be up for hours. If I were in there, he could usually fall asleep in about 30 minutes. I felt that his sleep was more important than my time even though I constantly second guessed myself knowing that it was not a good habit for him to have. He also frequently had nightmares, as has always been the case. He would often wake up in the middle of the night afraid because of a bad dream. He would dream of scary and frightening things. I know these dreams were not the result of watching TV shows because he didn't watch much TV. What he did watch was never scary because he did not like things like that. He didn't like sad movies either, especially when it involved animals. Neither did he play video games. His dreams seemed to come from nowhere but his own mind.

As the year came to a close, I knew something else needed to be done with the medicine. He was very defiant with me and disrespectful. He seemed upset and angry at every little thing. I felt that I had no influence or control over his behavior and I was so frustrated. I thought that I would really work on everything over the summer so fifth grade would be better. We started seeing a Christian counselor who came highly recommended. I also took Ethan off the Concerta. Once again we were back to thinking that maybe it wasn't a physical problem that he couldn't help but instead a behavioral problem that could be helped with a better plan. I started to use the *1, 2, 3, Magic* program and began to second guess all of my parenting techniques. I wanted to be consistent and knew how important it was, but I kept feeling like I couldn't be consistent with Ethan. I would literally have to have consequences for almost every minute of the day if I were to be consistent. Other people just couldn't understand what it was really like for us. Most thought that by using behavior modification techniques with consequences and rewards consistently, anyone's behavior would change. I found that the harder I tried to enforce consequences, the worse his behavior got. He started to be disrespectful and defiant. I started to wonder if he had Oppositional Defiance Disorder instead of ADHD. The only problem with that theory is that the research on it still pointed to a behavior that could be changed with a certain method and/or therapy. I figured at this point that I must be doing everything wrong.

Over the summer, Ethan had a bad fall in front of our house. He was running, as usual, and slipped on wet cement. He hit the back of his head and was screaming. I put him in the bath to warm him up and tried to speak with him. I noticed that he kept asking the same questions over and over again. He seemed to have lost his short term memory. I called the doctor's office and then took him to the emergency room. He was given the usual scans and tests. His memory began to return and we were told that he should be just fine. It was not recommended to have any further testing or treatment for the injury. He had a huge knot on his head and it gave us a big scare, but we returned home not thinking that it should have any effect on him in the future.

Pieces to the Puzzle

- Counted things like steps to a place, times to chew his food,
  ceiling tiles, etc…

- Struggling with peers

- Doesn't like to read

- Impulsive

- Cries easily

- Doesn't like himself

- Worried about what other kids think of him

- Empathetic, especially towards animals

- Loved to play the drums

- Risk taker

- Nightmares

- Aggression

Later Elementary School...

In third grade, I was in Mrs. King's class. She loved Jeff Gordon and NASCAR. My mom told me that I started taking medicine this year, but I don't remember that. I do remember that it was the year that we studied sharks! I wrote a report on the Lemon shark and made a large one out of cardboard. We also went to Sea World and slept over night there. It was a lot of fun. While we were there though, I got so mad at one of my friends for teasing me that I pulled his pants down. I almost got thrown out. We did a lot of fun things that year and I joined my mom's Odyssey of the Mind team.

In fourth grade, I was in Mrs. Macon's class. She was a nice teacher because she did not yell or get mad easily. I felt like she liked me. This is also the year we went to Sea Camp. Sea Camp was the best field trip ever. We went out in the ocean and went snorkeling and I saw a 6 foot barracuda. This was way better then going to school. I think my behavior was okay this year, but there are two things that I remember. One was that there was this kid that I hated. He was new to our school and only stayed for that one school year. He did weird things that made him annoying. Most people did not get along with him, but it was especially hard for me. The worst thing that happened to me was that I scratched a car's front bumper and I had to pay hundreds of dollars of my own money to fix it. We were at recess and a girl told me to do it and I did. I know not to listen to people when they tell me to do something wrong, but I did anyway. I don't know why.

I had to go to the hospital again during the summer between 4th and 5th grades. I was running and slipping on my sidewalk and then I fell. I hit the back of my head and couldn't remember things. It hurt a lot and I didn't like going to the hospital. It got better though.

Two cool things happened that summer. First, we got our dog, Mandy. My mom said we could get a Golden Retriever if we could find an adult one that we could afford. She was looking in the paper and suggested that we call vet offices. I sat with the yellow pages and called a lot of vet offices until I found one who said they knew of one needing a home. We called the older people and went to get her. She was free because they were too old to take care of her and just wanted a good home for her. The other thing that happened was that it was the summer we got hit with Hurricane Charley. We thought it was going to pass us, so we stayed home. At the last minute, it turned and hit Sanibel Island. We live very close to the Sanibel Causeway, so we got some damage too. We stayed in our hallway and bathroom with a mattress, just in case. It was a little scary, but exciting too.

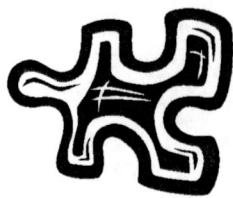

What Happened in Fifth Grade?

I was actually looking forward to Ethan entering fifth grade. I had taught that grade level for many years and enjoyed the curriculum and the children. I also knew that it was an exciting time in the children's lives. They are finally the oldest in the elementary school and they are beginning to be more independent from adults.

Unfortunately, fifth grade became the year that "all hell broke loose" for us. At the time I attributed the problems to several different factors. One was the attitude that Ethan had about his teacher and school in general. Another factor was that he was going through hormonal changes in his body that could make him more irritable. A third factor could have been that his medicine was changed again. This time it was Strattera, and I wondered if it was helping any symptoms at all. I would later find out that while all of those may have been factors in the problems, so could have been his recent head injury over the summer.

One of the first problems I noticed in fifth grade was the decline in his grades and work habits. Even though I had seen some initial signs of struggling, he had always been an A/B student, learned easily, and completed all of his assignments. I was concerned when I got reports of missing work and low scores. Ethan began to dread all school work this year. It went beyond the usual disinterest of an active boy. He actually loathed going to school and any work associated with it. This was especially hard for me, a teacher who loved learning. I ended up having to work with him at home on a daily basis to learn the information and complete the regular work, along with extra credit assignments. This took a toll on our relationship since it always was a conflict. He now saw me as mother, disciplinarian, and teacher. I think he felt oppressed in every way and he vented his frustration and anger all of the time.

Along with the school work, he also was frustrated with his teacher. Mr. Smith had a different teaching style than what Ethan was used to, especially coming from Mrs. Macon the year before. He wanted the students to be more responsible for their learning as well as for all of their materials. Ethan just felt that he wasn't being taught anything and completely floundered. He had trouble concentrating for the lecture style format of the lessons and never seemed to fully understand any of the material. Ethan also felt that he changed his mind and/or directions frequently which is something Ethan has a hard time with. Mr. Smith tried to have consistent consequences, like I had earlier, because Ethan seemed to spend a good deal of time with some form of punishment. Unfortunately, it all seemed to just spiral downward all year. The more he got in trouble, the more Ethan became defensive and disrespectful. Of course, as that happened, Mr. Smith needed to provide more consequences. I can relate to Mr. Smith's feelings of frustration as a teacher and how hard it is to deal with a challenging student, but I did not agree with some of his tactics he used with Ethan and feel that in some ways it made things worse. It was a good example of why teachers need to understand various problems and learn how to be better equipped in dealing with them.

Ethan had a lot of trouble with his classmates as well as the neighborhood children that year. He constantly told me that no one liked him and that other kids were talking about him and making fun of him. I knew in the past that some children would exclude him or put him down, but I didn't know if that was completely true of the situation this year or if it was just his perception. One day he actually asked the whole class to raise their hands if they hated him just to prove it to himself. Of course some of the kids did raise their hands either being silly or because they were frustrated with his behavior at the time too. He seemed to shift from victim to bully though in fifth grade. He began to treat one boy in particular very badly. This was a student who had been in Ethan's classes since they were in preschool. I didn't know about it until it had been going on awhile and his mother got in touch with me. I was horrified. How could my child be mistreating someone this badly, especially when I knew how empathetic and considerate he could be? I tried everything I knew to do to stop it. We all met together with the teacher in order to get it out in the open. We had the boys meet with the school counselor. I had Ethan's private counselor work with him on it. I asked for reports from the boy and his mother and if Ethan did something mean, he was punished at home. I think there were times when things got better, but I don't think it ever really ended. That student ended up leaving our school when fifth grade ended. I am still so ashamed of Ethan's behavior and choices and unfortunately that wasn't the end of it.

During fifth grade, we spent a lot of time in professional offices. He started off back at the pediatrician's office, where he was started on Strattera because it just seemed like the Concerta wasn't helping anymore. Even though this is not classified as a stimulant, it is still being used to treat ADHD. He was also still seeing the same Christian counselor. Since things seemed to be getting worse instead of better, I figured I needed to do something different once again. Later in the school year, the pediatrician prescribed Clonidine, along with the Strattera, which he tried for a short while. I don't really remember what the reason was that we discontinued that medication. I finally decided it was time to see a psychiatrist because there was nothing anyone else could do. I went to see a psychiatrist because I kept thinking that nothing we have tried so far has seemed to help, so maybe it is something that is more physical in nature. Our insurance would pay for only a few psychiatrists in our area, so I found one willing to see a child. His name was Dr. Abernathy and I was so disappointed when we got in to see him. He did not want any prior history of Ethan, nor was I allowed to ask any questions. He was very unfriendly and even a bit shady. He offered to give Ethan a prescription for some anti depressant, which I took but never filled. I felt so ill at ease with him that we never went back. Fortunately, I was able to have Ethan seen by Dr. Roy who is a well known child psychiatrist in town. It was hard to get the appointment and he is not covered by our insurance, but having a good professional on your team is priceless. He basically heard all the history and also seemed to think ADHD was the most likely problem. He wanted Ethan to continue on the Strattera for the time being. He also recommended a few counselors and that is how we began seeing Susan Black.

Ethan was thrilled with the new counselor, Susan Black. She was a total advocate for him and he loved the way that felt. She also felt sure that he had ADHD and had been treated as though he didn't for too many years. She made me realize that I had not been fair at times with my expectations of him and the same was true for the school. She often reminded me that his limitations were real and were what was frustrating him so much. She said that he was the most frustrated ten year-old she had ever seen. Susan thought that he needed accommodations in school so it would not be so hard for him. She was very upset with his current teacher and she felt that he was not helping Ethan at all. Susan even felt that there was a possibility that Ethan had a language learning disability because of his difficulty retelling a story and some of his word choice. Susan felt that the rigorous demands of a school like St. Matthew was probably not the best learning environment for him. I had mixed feelings because even though I knew he was currently struggling, I also knew what kind of a student he had always been. He had been perfectly capable of performing like the other students for all of those years, so I was confused as to just what had happened.

Hearing all of these things was heart breaking and confusing to me. It just seemed to make no sense. I would go back over the same truths; he was a great kid, he learned so easily, he had so many good qualities, I had worked so hard to parent him correctly, he is very much loved, we have seen professionals, etc. However, I also knew what a typical day for him was like. He couldn't wake up in the morning, so it always resulted in an argument before school. He also might have trouble finding the "right" clothes to wear once he was up. He would be mad the whole way to school and be disrespectful to me. In school, he would have conflicts with peers and trouble paying attention in class. He would usually be reprimanded in some way. After school he would tell me that none of the kids like him and we fought trying to get homework completed. He didn't want to do it and it seemed he was not able to complete it correctly a lot of the time. Many times he was serving some kind of punishment because of a behavior problem during school. He would complain about dinner and usually slam things around at some point in the evening over something he would be mad about. Trying to go to bed would result in more arguments as he would try excuses to prolong his bed time. Once in bed, he couldn't fall asleep. I would go in his room to help him go to sleep and he would play around, say mean things, etc. until I would leave. Then he would scream and have a fit until I would go back in there until he fell asleep an hour later. Each day was torture for both of us. I was certain that every household did not operate in this manner. Something had to be wrong; I just didn't know what it was.

There is one thing that Susan spoke with me about that still resonates with me. It is that she felt I needed to be more of a soft spot for Ethan to fall on instead of the warden who made sure everything was completed up to par. She explained that Ethan would need to be able to speak with me about problems and feel that he was loved unconditionally, and that in order for that to happen I needed to be a different kind of parent. She suggested the *Love and Logic* books/materials and of course I bought a few of them to read. It all made good sense and once again I tried really hard to be the kind of parent Ethan needed me to be. This time however, some of it worked. I realized that it was very important for me to stay calm, use a soothing voice, to allow him to make more decisions on his own, and give him his independence in certain ways. I also made much more of an effort to let him know how much I loved him and to be that soft spot for him to land. These things have helped to make our relationship better and to keep our household calmer.

We did what we could to get through the end of that school year. We were both frazzled and emotionally drained. It would have been best to probably go away to some remote island and just unwind for a month or so. But no, we had to take two stimulating, people intensive trips at the end of that fifth grade year.

I coached two Odyssey of the Mind teams during that school year. It is a very time consuming program, even though I think it is an incredible opportunity for all those involved. Our teams work very hard during the whole school year and most stay together over many years. This year was particularly exciting because both of the teams had qualified for the World Finals in Colorado. Ethan was a member on the elementary team. He had mixed feelings about the whole program. I had been a coach since he was three and so he had always looked forward to being on my team. He liked the whole idea of the program and was very good at building things (mostly on his own though). What was challenging for him was the fact that it required a lot of time, work, and self discipline which were all things that he struggled with. He also liked the people on our team, but still ended up in arguments many times and found himself frustrated trying to cooperate with others. He also liked being around me when it was just the two of us, but he did not like me in a teacher or coach role and tended to seek attention which contributed to our tense relationship as well.

So it was the end of May and both teams, and their parents were all going to Colorado. It was tiring and we were already dragging at this time of the year. There were many small conflicts as well as excitement all around us. I remember that one of the eighth grade girls was teasing Ethan about a girl liking him and he became very mad and embarrassed. He hit the girl to get back at her and then her mother was outraged. It was not a pleasant experience. But Colorado was beautiful, most of us got along well, and Ethan's team won 2nd place for their problem in that division. We even rented cars to go up to the Rocky Mountains and were caught in a snow storm. It was incredibly beautiful and a wonderful time for us. Ethan had never seen snow before so he loved it for awhile and then ended up too wet and cold to a point that he got upset and cried for a while.

Even though we were physically exhausted and in much need of rest, the following week we left for Europe with our school's travel club. We had reserved our spot the previous summer and had been paying for it all year. It was an incredible opportunity for our family. My ticket was free as a chaperone and the rest of the family got an employee discount. Europe was fabulous and our tour group was great. We visited Italy, Germany, Austria, and Switzerland in 10 days. We were very busy and excited much of the time. At the beginning of our trip, Ethan had a hard time. This was especially true in the evenings. I think he was too tired and over stimulated. He would be angry, argumentative, and stubborn. There were several nights when I would take him back to the room early in order to get him to sleep. Early on in the trip we stayed in Venice, Italy. I had to bring Ethan upstairs early and he went into the bathroom. The next thing I knew, he had opened the window and was dangling out of it threatening to jump because he was mad. I managed to coax him back in the room but it remained an issue several times throughout the trip. At this time, he was not on any medication and I was about at the end of my rope. I am glad we took the trip, but wish it could have been a little easier for Ethan. He still thinks of it as one of the best times he has ever had and I'm glad his memory of it was good.

I was determined to get to the bottom of this situation over the summer. For many years I struggled with feeling that I wasn't parenting correctly. How could I help not to? Professionals, and even my own family and friends, had often given me advice about what I should be doing differently. I even heard comments about if someone else were raising him, he would be different. None of my siblings have any children of their own, so you can only imagine how frustrated I felt hearing those kinds of remarks from them. I also heard things about boys being boys and that Ethan and I had a personality conflict. From time to time, I also dealt with the idea that Ethan's issues stemmed from not having a stable father in his life. While I understood that and agreed that it made it harder for Ethan, I still felt that his problems had always been present and did not start after our divorce. I have tried to be open and honest with Ethan in regards to his father. I have allowed their relationship to continue as long as Ethan's safety was foremost. I knew Ethan wished things were different with his dad, but I also knew that I had to keep searching for a different answer instead of getting stuck on that situational answer.

As we continued to see Dr. Roy and Susan Black, we also added Dr. Norris to our list that summer. I had done some research on my own about mood disorders and I felt that there was a chance that Ethan may be struggling with one. Susan Black was still curious about a learning disability and he was still being seen as an ADHD patient from everyone. Dr. Norris did some testing on Ethan that summer. Basically the results showed that his IQ fell within the above average range and there was no learning disability. She also saw ADHD tendencies and some mood problems. She thought it would be helpful for him to see a male therapist in order to help him with the feelings he had about his father and our divorce. Dr. Norris was undecided about St. Matthew as it was a place where he felt comfortable and safe as well as a place that caused him much stress and frustration. One area which most concerned me was that his working memory score was the lowest score (average range) and he had always had such a great memory that it shocked me to see that. When Dr. Roy saw it, he said that if Ethan had been on medication, the score would have been higher. He thought it was a result of ADHD.

Pieces to the Puzzle

- Angry

- Acts as though threatened

- Paranoid about what others think or say

- Low tolerance level

- Not compliant

- Negative perception of events or people

- Felt hopeless about his situation

- Forgetfulness

- Verbally hurtful

- Frustrated

- Struggling with academics

- Unfocused and poor concentration

- Hyper

- Moody

- Easily over stimulated

- Holds grudges

- Becomes stressed easily

Fifth Grade...

In fifth grade, my teacher was Mr. Smith. I didn't really like the type of teacher that he was. He talked a lot when he was teaching and it was hard to keep concentrating on what he was saying. It was very boring. My grades were worse than usual. I had to do a lot of extra credit that year to keep making good grades. I did not get along with him. He made me write essays like crazy and miss recess. I had to sit out in the hallway sometimes and even went to the principal's office a few times. Sometimes he even got the other kids in my class to help keep me paying attention. I remember one time that I had to look at the board and if I didn't, all of the other students had to point at me. I was really embarrassed. My behavior wasn't very good, but neither was his towards me. I was angry almost every day. I hated going to school.

I felt like nobody liked me and I didn't like myself either. I know I had a few friends in my class, but I can't remember very many good times. I was good friends with Sam, Lori, and Irwin but there were other kids that I got along with okay too. The few good times I had are covered up by the bad times I had with Mr. Smith and another student in my class. The other student had been in my class every year since I was four. He was different from most other kids. I think that he acted like he knew everything and he was annoying to me. For some reason his very existence bothered me. I made fun of him and called him names. I was rude and mean to him. It made me feel like I over powered him. The other kids laughed and carried on with me. Lots of kids made fun of him but I was the one that got in trouble for it. I ended up getting in a lot of trouble with my mom over it, but I just couldn't seem to leave him alone because he bothered me so much.

The best part of fifth grade was that I got to play on the St. Matthew soccer team. I had been playing with the same organization since kindergarten and I had looked forward to finally playing for our school. My friends were on the team too and we were pretty good. Mr. Solonbrock, one of my friend's dad, was our coach.

My mom started taking me to doctors and counselors. I hated going. I know I was taking some kind of medicine, but don't remember much about it except that I didn't care that I took it. Dr. Kim was a counselor that we saw for a little while. I liked his boat but he didn't really help me at all. We started seeing Susan Black after that. She was a lot better. She was cool and she liked me. She didn't like what Mr. Smith was doing either and made me feel like I was right. We even saw this one weird psychiatrist named Dr. Abernathy. My mom thought he was weird too, so we never went back. It was in the middle of 5th grade that I started seeing Dr. Roy, another psychiatrist. He was much better than the other one. I wanted to be happier and have fun, but nothing was helping. Each day just seemed to get worse. I wanted to run away from home and I wanted to be dead or just gone. Susan Black told me that if I ever really ran away from home to look for signs that say safe place, like at McDonald's. She said I should go to one of those and ask for help.

I was on my mom's Odyssey of the Mind team for the third year. We were pretty good, but it was hard work and took a lot of time and I hated that part. I built a big tree and a highway sign. I had wanted to quit this year, but I liked going to the competitions. That year we made it to World Finals in Colorado where we took 2nd place in our problem and division. I liked the place we stayed and we had a lot of fun there. One day we rented cars and went up to the Rocky Mountains. We were 2.3 miles above sea level and it was snowing. It was weird because it was the end of May and 80 degrees Fahrenheit in Boulder. It was the first time that I saw snow.

That summer our family went to Europe with other people from St. Matthew. It took eleven hours to get there. There were thirty people in our school group. We went to four countries: Italy, Austria, Germany, and Switzerland. Some of my favorite things were going up Mt. Pilatus in Switzerland and going through the salt mine in Germany. I became good friends with the bus driver, Giuseppe. He drove us all around and was pretty funny. It was the best vacation we ever had. I know I got into trouble and had to go to our room early a few nights, but I don't remember what I did or why I was in trouble.

I also had some more testing done over the summer. I didn't like going to Dr. Norris because she was different. It was boring and the tests were pretty easy. I was glad when it was over and I could just enjoy my summer. I love summers because there is no school or homework. I get a lot of playtime and get to be outside most of the day.

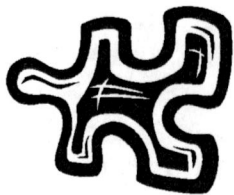

Middle School...

I decided to keep Ethan at St. Matthew for middle school. One reason was because that was where I worked and it seemed like a good idea to keep Ethan close by. Another reason was because he had been there since he was three. It was like a home away from home for us. It was what he knew and felt comfortable with even though the academic pace was fast and expectations were high. I had spoken to Mr. Zoelle, the principal, at length about our situation and he was willing to work with us to help make it work for Ethan. I had already decided that even though I would help Ethan to study and complete homework, I was not going to be overly demanding or set my expectations too high. I didn't know of a school that would be better for him. I felt that it was a safe place for him because everyone knew him and I hoped would care for him no matter he did. I just wanted it to work out for him at our school and for us to figure out what the root of the problems was.

Ethan was placed in Mrs. Lane's home room because I was the home room teacher for the other sixth grade class. She and I were good friends and she already knew Ethan's history. As a matter of fact, she was the person who spoke to me about the possibility of bipolar a year or so earlier and she is the one who noticed Ethan's high anxiety level and put a name on it for me during the sixth grade school year. Ethan was excited to start middle school and seemed ready to go back to St. Matthew.

Dr. Roy was willing to prescribe different types of medications that year in order to better understand what was going on with Ethan and find him some relief. At first, he tried Imipramine which is a tricyclic antidepressant. This seemed to make him more hyper and it didn't last long. The next medication we tried was Depakote which is considered a mood stabilizer. At first it seemed very positive. Ethan was much happier and we were all very excited. Shortly after the positive effects, the tiredness set in. He was falling asleep in class, had a hard time keeping up with his studies, and had no energy for anything. It was soccer season for Ethan and even though he loved to play, he had no energy. He couldn't even run the lap around the track. He was used to being fast and quick with the ball and now he struggled to even play. The other team mates gave him a hard time because they just thought he was being lazy. The coach knew and understood, but couldn't help him too much. I felt bad for him and discussed it with Dr. Roy who agreed it was not going to work for him.

One interesting thing I learned about these medicines was that they were not the kind that you start and stop instantly, like the stimulants used for ADHD. Generally, the medication needs to be started at a low dose and then gradually increased until you reach a therapeutic level. If it is found to not be effective, then the medication is slowly and gradually decreased. The whole process can take weeks and even months. During that time, the side effects can be hard to deal with and/or the behavior can remain the same and at times worsen.

While Ethan was on Depakote, he became more irritable than usual because of the tiredness. He was snapping at classmates, was extremely rude to me in school, and was becoming quite unhappy again. He seemed to be having an especially hard time with the girls in his class. I wondered then if it had anything to do with him viewing females as the weaker sex and finding them easier targets. He was acting like a bully again which now I look at as a defense mechanism he uses to cover for his own insecurities. He tries to control everything and everyone around him when he feels himself being out of control. Because he hates when others don't like him and hates to be in trouble, his behaviors sent him spiraling down.

In November, he switched medicines and tried Lithobid which is also a mood stabilizer from lithium. This is considered the "gold standard" of mood stabilizers so I was sure that it would work. We knew it could take a long time to get up to the therapeutic dose and even longer before we might see the positive results we were hoping for. He had regular blood draws before school to check the levels and he was so good about having that done. He never complained. Unfortunately, things got worse for him during December.

Similar to last school year, Ethan had one particular target in sixth grade. This time it was a girl in his class. He somehow was annoyed by her behavior and felt the need to dominate over her. It didn't help that she was often picked on by other classmates, especially behind her back. That just fueled Ethan's fire toward her and he became the spokesperson against her for the entire sixth grade. As I learned more about it, I became increasingly concerned and embarrassed. I tried the same tactics as the year before with Ethan, but I knew it was not the answer. The girl's parents were of course very unhappy and concerned. Since it is a small school where everyone knows each other, I felt that he was becoming the topic of conversation at many people's dinner table. There was nothing good about the situation.

Just as Ethan's behaviors were worse, so were his emotions. By December, he hated everything again, including himself. He spoke about dying and how everything would be better if he were not here. Death came up almost daily and it was very scary to me. I knew that it was not normal for children to bring that up as an option for anything. He spent most of his time either angry or sad and that didn't work well with the demands of school.

Over Christmas vacation Ethan became very upset. It was a combination of things. He had wanted a radio in his room and was frustrated that none of the stations would come in clearly. He tried several different stereos that he got for Christmas and we couldn't get any of them to work correctly. He was also upset about his father's situation. He wanted to have a close relationship with him and he wanted his dad to be doing better than he was at the time. He was also just generally sad and angry as I stated earlier. Something snapped in him one evening when I was here alone with him. He was so angry that he took a bat and started hitting things in his room. I finally managed to get the bat away from him and I went to hide it. When I returned, he had a knife from his pocket knife collection out and was stabbing his science fair project board. It totally scared me. I thought then that it would be so easy for him to stab me with his anger being out of control. I don't even remember how, but I convinced him to give me the knife. After twenty minutes or so, he was back to normal like nothing had ever happened. Needless to say, I removed all the bats and knives from his room that night and he still does not have them to this day.

I learned something that night though. I learned that nothing was more important to me than helping my son to get better. I knew then that I would do whatever it took to find the answers and make his life better. The last thing I wanted was to make things worse for him. The next year was going to be one of many hard decisions and changes for us.

I was terribly worried about losing the son I had. It was harder to see the side of him that was loving, empathetic, caring, helpful, smart, outgoing, etc… He was being replaced by someone I hardly knew, and frankly, didn't care to know.

So, I made a decision and in January I withdrew Ethan from St. Matthew and enrolled him in a public middle school. It wasn't that I thought the school was a great place for him, it was more of the fact that I needed a quick change and it was important to find out what would happen in that type of school. I wanted Ethan away from the girl who he was picking on and away from all the people at St. Matthew who were now talking about him. I stayed working there in my same position even though it was extremely hard for me to see all of his friends each day. One parent from St. Matthew called me when she realized Ethan had withdrawn. I was thankful for that, but saddened by the fact that no one else even asked me about it at the time. How could he attend school and birthday parties for nine years with these families and not have anyone show concern about him or his absence? That crushed me since I was already vulnerable to my emotions.

The first nine weeks he attended Lincoln Middle School went pretty smoothly. Just avoiding the daily fight to get him out of bed each morning was an immediate help. He made good grades and met lots of girls who liked him. He felt better about himself. There was one incident that landed him in internal suspension though. He said that a boy pushed him down, so he got up and pushed him slightly back. Since both boys were physical, they both were put in IS. I don't know what events led up to original push and of course Ethan states that he didn't do anything. Other than that, school progressed normally and I was just trying to get us through the school year without incident so I could try to figure out my next plan over the summer.

In one of our visits with Dr. Roy, I mentioned that even though school seemed to be going well, Ethan still became angry easily and was still being disrespectful and uncooperative with me at home. We also spoke in length about his anxieties which sometimes prevented him from living normally. I had done some research and could understand a little more of the reasoning behind some of Ethan's negative behavior. He had fears of being embarrassed and not liked by other kids his age. They were more than typical apprehensions and he tried to hide them by showing behavior that was just the opposite of how he felt inside. He would over compensate for his insecurities and fears. He often acted as if he was defensive and was not going to let people hurt him. The only problem was I wasn't convinced people were hurting him. It may have been more of a false perception or taking silly comments too seriously. It was like he was wearing filtered glasses that distorted his perceptions. At any rate, Dr. Roy decided to try Paxil (an anti depressant/anxiety medication) along with the Lithobid.

This proved to be a big mistake. At first, it seemed to be a wonderful medicine for him. Almost instantly Ethan seemed happier and easier to get along with. He was more of his normally loving self and helpful around the house. I was actually very excited about the results. Ethan was excited as well. He began talking a lot more and showed more excitement than usual. As the medication set in over a few weeks, we noticed that Ethan was actually very hyper and was engaging in more risky behaviors than usual. He was extra talkative and active. He was running and jumping all over the place and even tried to roller blade off of the roof of a house. I let Dr. Roy know what was going on and he first tried to add an ADHD medicine to the mix called Focalin, but there was no change. We then made the decision to take him off the Paxil, so he was weaned slowly off of it. During the few weeks that he was on Paxil at school, he started getting in all sorts of trouble at school. He was talking in class and at lunch too much, he stopped doing his school work, and he was having confrontations with other students. He even got into trouble on the bus which was his favorite part of going to public school. When I spoke to the principal about what was going on, she suggested that we try using the homebound program since it was a medical problem and not very fair to him to get into trouble for a medication side effect. I agreed and he finished the last quarter of sixth grade at home with a homebound teacher.

He was still taking Lithobid and Focalin and still having mood problems even though he was at home. It was frustrating to me that Paxil had made a positive difference that we no longer saw. So, Dr. Roy suggested that we try Zoloft. He said that it is easier to control the dose of Zoloft and felt that maybe a tiny bit would give us the positive results without the negative side effects. He also took him off the Focalin, so we were trying Lithobid plus a tiny bit of Zoloft. It wasn't perfect and neither was Ethan's behavior, but without the stress of school, things were better. It was still a very difficult time for our family though. I was missing a lot of work. Thank goodness the principal, Mr. Zoelle, was understanding and tried to work with me on everything. My husband, Jim, was having some parenting struggles of his own and his mother passed away during this time as well. Both of us were worn out physically and emotionally while we were still trying to support each other. Once again I found myself just trying to make it to the end of another school year to try to figure out a new plan over the summer. Not only was it a stressful time, I also found it to be sort of a weird or secretive situation. To most people on the outside, our family seemed completely normal. Even for my friends, family, and coworkers who knew there were struggles had never seen our real world. My husband didn't even get to see a lot of the knock down, drag out explosions. Ethan's rages and hateful talk were saved for me in the safety of our home or he whispered things so no one can hear them but me. This, I have since learned, is common for children like Ethan. They some-how manage to hold in their emotions in front of other people, but at home they can let their guard down and release their fears and stress in a safe place. It is also very common for the mother to get the worst of their behavior. Since I didn't know that at the time, I worried that people thought I was just too stressed out or exag-gerating the situation. I knew our lives were out of control and that we needed help. Thank goodness I had already taken a new step towards solving this situation.

PIECES OF THE PUZZLE

- Irritable
- Uncooperative
- Aggressive
- Agitated
- Defiant
- Unhappy
- Worried
- Manic
- Stimulants and antidepressants have had opposite effects on him
- Impatient
- Poor judgment
- Over reactive
- Social anxieties
- Conflict seeking
- Memory problems
- Short fuse
- Holds grudges
- Wanted things done a certain way
- Repetitive thoughts

Middle School...

I stayed at St. Matthew for middle school because it is a school that has grades PreK-3 all the way through eighth grade. My homeroom teacher was Mrs. Lane because my mom was the other 6th grade homeroom teacher and I couldn't be in her class. I had some friends in my class, but I also had kids I didn't get along with. The boy I didn't get along with in fifth grade went to another school, but now there was a girl in my class that bothered me. The way she did things bothered me. It was like she thought she knew everything and always had to say it. I called her names and was mean to her because it made me feel like I had more power over her. I don't know why I needed to feel that way, but I still do. I don't like it when kids think they know it all and they really don't or when kids brag a lot. They should just be quiet about what they know or can do.

I was still seeing Dr. Roy and Susan Black and I was trying some new types of medicine. The medicine I was on at the beginning of the school year made me very tired. I fell asleep in class sometimes and I was irritable. I was on the soccer team again, but I was so tired that I could barely run and play. I didn't like being so tired and was glad when I quit taking that medicine. I tried another kind and with that one I had to have my blood drawn on some mornings. I didn't mind that though. Susan Black talked to me about my anger and getting along with other kids. She was nice, but I got to where I didn't want to go anymore. I just wanted to go home and play.

In January, I changed schools. I went to Lincoln Middle School which is a public school. My mom let me change because I was so mad all of the time and wasn't getting along with some kids at school. Dr. Roy and Susan Black thought it might help too because St. Matthew is kind of a hard school. Lincoln was alright, but it was a big school. There were a lot of different people in the school that I wasn't used to. About a month or two after I got there I got in trouble and got an IS (internal suspension). A kid said I made a face at him and he pushed me down. I got up and barely pushed him back but we both got in trouble. I noticed that the kids did a lot more bad things at that school than at St. Matthew. I did make some friends there though and I really liked riding a school bus. I had always wanted to do that.

The quarter went by pretty fast and I made A's and B's. I even made the honor roll. It was around the start of the next quarter that I had to take another medicine along with the one I was already taking. For the next 4 weeks I got into a lot of trouble at school for talking, fighting, and fooling around. I got in trouble one day and my mom never sent me back to Lincoln. I was supposed to have another IS on the day I returned. I wonder if I ever go back to public school if I will have to serve it. I finished the school year at home with a homebound teacher. I liked being at home and I got good grades. I also stopped taking the new medicine and again tried another one.

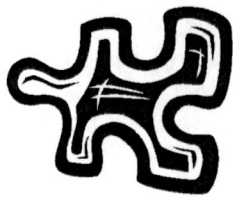

The Brain Piece...

During the school year, I had seen something interesting on the Dr. Phil show two different times. The first time planted a seed. The second time sealed the deal. He had a company called Brain Matters, Inc. on the show explaining a relatively new technology to help understand neurological disorders. It is called SPECT (Single Photon Emission Computed Tomography) imaging and it primarily shows the blood flow and metabolism in the brain which determines how each area is functioning at rest and then when concentrating or working. It is different than the typical brain imaging studies like MRI and CT that are used in most hospitals as it is not just looking at structural brain abnormalities, but on the actual workings of the brain. It was helping doctors to recognize brain patterns associated with disorders like Aspergers, OCD, ADHD, and bipolar. I did some of my own research and determined that if I didn't have this done for Ethan, I would never be able to rest. I thought that it was important to actually use an objective tool as opposed to just a subjective person's opinion. I made an appointment for him in Denver for the beginning of May. It would be worth the cost and trip to finally get a chance to see what is going on inside of his brain.

Ethan did great in Denver and we had a nice time together. I was extremely pleased with the whole process and with all of the people at Brain Matters. The scan was done twice on two different days. The first time he was asked to concentrate on a computer game while a nuclear medicine was placed in his blood stream. He then had to lie down for about 16 minutes while a special camera took pictures of his brain. He then came back another day and did the same thing except his brain was at rest. We came back home afterwards and waited for the results. They had an experienced and trained doctor read the scans to interpret the patterns seen in Ethan's brain. They called us to explain the initial findings and then sent a notebook with all of the results and photos. Once we had time to review it all, they called again for an hour consultation to make sure we understood everything. Dr. Roy even got a phone call from the doctor in Denver, Dr. Hendren, along with his own copy of the results.

The findings were amazing to me and I felt that knowing what was going on in his brain would surely help in finding the right medicine. The pattern of activity they saw in Ethan's prefrontal cortex was not one associated with ADHD. In fact, his brain showed the opposite pattern. Normally with ADHD there would be a decreased blood flow in the prefrontal cortex, especially during concentration, but Ethan's did not show that at all, ruling out the possibility of having ADHD. After having a tool like this, it is hard to believe that the majority of the children are still being diagnosed from a subjective checklist created by people. They also found that a few areas showed an increased blood flow pattern. Those areas were the limbic system, the basal ganglia, and the cingulate gyrus. This may all stem from a common problem or they could result from different disorders, I am not sure. These areas are responsible for mood, anxiety, and cognitive flexibility respectfully. All of these have been issues for Ethan. What else they found really took me by surprise though. They said that his temporal lobes had been damaged from some sort of traumatic brain injury. Even though SPECT scans are still questioned for psychiatric purposes, they are completely supported for use with traumatic brain injury as well as other conditions so I knew that there were no mistakes about their finding of TBI. I was not prepared to hear that and I couldn't figure out what happened for a little while. They told me that the brain is very soft while it sits within a very hard, spiny shell. It appeared that an equal force would have occurred to the point of both of his temporal lobes sloshing around inside the skull in the same manner. It must have been the fall he had the summer before fifth grade because it was a direct hit to the back of his head and resulted in short term memory loss. Brain Matters explained to me that the temporal lobes are mostly responsible for language, memory, temper, musical ability, and spiritual beliefs. These are all things Ethan had struggled with since the accident.

Of course, I did more research on my own and was surprised by all the things I learned. Brain damage is very common although not many people realize it. Doctors don't even seem to be overly concerned about it. It made me angry that the doctors at the hospital didn't send us to a specialist or let me know in some way that there was a possibility of permanent damage. I would have made sure he had gotten treatment to prevent as much damage as possible. Brain Matters said that his temporal lobes are actually better when he concentrates because the brain has tried to make new connections to correct the damage that was done. I am convinced that we could have made it even better had we known to do something intentional to help it repair itself. The more I thought about everything, the more I realized that this fall could have really contributed to a lot of our frustrations lately. Ethan's temper had certainly gotten worse since the fall and so had his memory and language skills. I think that is what Susan Black had seen when she worked with him and thought it was a language disability. I also believe that Ethan was more frustrated at school because he was used to having a superior memory and good language skills. When those were weakened, it made school work more difficult and thus created a situation he could not understand or control. Amazingly enough, even his interest in music and religion waned after his fall. What might appear to be normal adolescent changes or rebellion, I believe to be partially a result of his injury. When I read case histories of people with TBI, it really made me understand the idea more than I had before. It is remarkable how much correlation there is between the health of the brain and everyday life.

All of the information about the brain was so helpful that I continued to read more about it and possible treatments. Dr. Daniel Amen may be considered as the doctor who pioneered SPECT scan use for psychiatric purposes. He has a great web site (www.amen-clinics.com) and has a few clinics around the country. He has also written some great books. If I had my way, everyone would read some of them. My favorite so far is, *Change Your Brain Change Your Life*. It confirmed my suspicion that treatment for the brain is possible, however it is also complicated. Treatment not only involves medicine, but there are other aspects such as nutrition, daily life, therapy, and music.

As far as medicine goes, Brain Matters made it clear that Ethan should not be taking stimulants or activating medicines because his brain was already too active. Those are the medicines usually prescribed for ADHD, depression, and anxiety. That is the reason that so many of the medicines Ethan had already been on had failed, and possibly even had made things worse. While he had the scan done he was taking Lithobid and a tiny bit of Zoloft. They said that it was possible that the Zoloft was increasing the activity in the brain and to discontinue that. They also felt that the Lithobid was not working enough for him because of all the activity showing up in the photos. They suggested we try a different mood stabilizer, one that was considered an anticonvulsant which would possibly help the temporal lobes at the same time. First, the other medicine had to be reduced and then finally removed.

In June of 2006, Ethan turned twelve years old, was diagnosed with a possible cyclic mood disorder (bipolar) and TBI, and began taking another medicine called Trileptal. It was great to have an answer, but at the same time it was hard to deal with it. It felt like a death of sorts. My dream, not only for Ethan, but for our carefree life was altered significantly. I knew that some people with bipolar can lead normal lives, but I also knew that it is hard work to get it that stable.

In spite of the concerns, I was determined to be optimistic and not to give up. I was sure that over the summer all of our problems would be resolved. I had done my research. A SPECT scan helped provide the missing pieces that were necessary to solve the mystery of his behavior. I had conferred with other parents on an online support group with www.bpkids.org. The medication seemed to be a perfect fit for him and was supposed to work.

SPECT Scan...

I went to Colorado for a SPECT scan. It is this thing where they put stuff in my vein and then I have to lay still for 16 minutes while a camera rotates around my head taking like a hundred pictures of my brain. I couldn't have caffeine for almost a week while we were doing the scans. It was really hard for me and I couldn't wait until I finally got to have chocolate and soda when I was finished. We stayed at the Holiday Inn Select while we were there. It was cool. It had a heated indoor pool. I met Katie and Rachael who worked at the front desk. I hung out with them a lot and when we had to go home I didn't like leaving. They got me a card and a bunch of gum. I kept the card and some things from the hotel to remember them. I would like to go back there one day.

The scan showed that I have bipolar, which is a mood disorder, and anxiety. The pictures showed different colors in my brain. The colors that I had meant that there was more blood than is usual. It also showed that my temporal lobes were damaged. It must have been from the fall I had on the sidewalk a couple of years before the scan was done. I think it was a good idea to have had the scan done because we found out what was wrong.

The doctor said to stop taking the medicines I was on and to try Trileptal. I took it all summer long and into the fall but it wasn't helping me. I got double vision sometimes with it though.

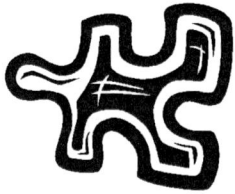

Picking Up the Pieces...

As the summer started to draw to an end, I was confronted with the possibility that the medicine may not be working. If it wasn't, would he be ready to go back to school? If so, which school? It was again time for drastic decisions to be made. Jim and I conferred, I prayed, I thought, I spoke to others about the possibilities, and then I started to look for different employment. I felt that sending Ethan back to school before a medication was in place would be setting him up for failure. I also knew that our family was not set up financially to do with out my paycheck. I again spoke with our principal about our predicament. He was still supportive and helped me work out some of the details. He was willing to allow me to take a leave of absence for one semester or one school year. He even kept me working part time as a consultant for the teacher taking my place and for students with special needs in the school. That situation allowed me to take a large leap of faith and keep Ethan home from school.

When August rolled around Ethan and I stayed home to complete school and work on a treatment plan for him. I ended up finding a few different part time jobs to help with some income. I consulted for St. Matthew, worked for the university as an intern supervisor and as a mentor for beginning teachers in the county, and even tied fish hooks at home for a deep sea fishing boat. They all had flexible hours and a work at home component that allowed me to spend the majority of my time with Ethan. Even during this time, God provided me with information and connections that would continue to help me along my journey. I met many people, organizations, and groups of people that have somehow helped me to understand Ethan's needs more and have helped to pave the way for my being able to advocate for his disorder. I enrolled Ethan in a math class with Florida Virtual School and then we did other school related activities as we could. I think our favorite was going to Discovery Cove where we swam with dolphins. It was something we both really wanted to do and it was a way of building our relationship back up and making positive memories. Writing this book was another one of our home school activities. I have enjoyed it, but Ethan had difficulty with it at times. When we started, he was not stable and often refused to write. When he did write, it was just a small amount. He also became frustrated trying to remember things from the past and then to explain some of his feelings. We looked at photos to help his memory and I asked questions to help him put his thoughts into words.

Besides the medicine, I also looked into other possible treatments for him. One type of treatment that is highly recommended is to make lifestyle changes. Any kind of stress can trigger emotional outbursts in people with bipolar so we strived to simplify our home life. We cut back on the amount of activities we were involved with so there were fewer commitments of our time and thoughts. We also changed some of our expectations as far as Ethan's responsibilities and consequences. I really tried to grow our personal relationship during this time as well. Cognitive Behavior Therapy is another suggested treatment. Our counselor, Susan Black, is certified in it but we decided to wait and start that after Ethan is stable for awhile because I think it will be more effective at that point. I would have loved to have changed his diet and eating habits but he is adamant that he won't do that. I decided to let go of that idea in hopes that as he becomes more stable and better educated on the disorder, maybe he will be more willing to change his eating habits to be healthier. I did get him started back into music a little more with my brother because that is another great therapy for the brain. I really miss his musical interest and am hoping he regains that.

While home, I decided to have Ethan's language skills tested again because of the temporal lobe damage and Susan Black's concerns. I took him to a speech therapist, and she did a series of tests with him. Because his scores were mostly in the average range, she concluded that he showed no signs of a disability nor did he need any services from her. There were a few lower scores which could be accounted for in various ways such as tiredness from a medication. I believe that had he taken these tests a few years ago, his scores would have been much higher. The combination of bipolar disorder and traumatic brain injury can certainly reduce a person's cognitive abilities.

After few months had passed, Ethan stopped taking Trileptal. Even though we stayed with it a long time, it never seemed to do the trick. It was sad for me to let go of the hope that medicine held. Sometimes I feel like I have had to bury so many dreams along the way, I just didn't want another disappointment.

Thank goodness we went to the next medicine that Dr. Roy and Dr. Hendren thought to try though. It was Seroquel, which is considered an atypical antipsychotic. He had never been on that class of medications before, but there had been some positive talk lately about this one. There was an immediate difference in Ethan from the first dose he tried. We increased the dose very slowly, but there was a continual improvement along the way. Ethan said that he felt happier and it showed. He didn't mention death over the first few months of taking the medicine. He smiled more and was easier to be around. His overall mood was more positive and he started getting much better sleep. He felt better about himself and there hadn't been any negative side effects to go along with the positive ones.

One incident really stands out for me during this time. I was away from the house some mornings observing my interns and Ethan usually stayed home and did some school work after he woke up. One day I came home to find a gift wrapped and propped inside the front door. I opened the package that was addressed to me and found an 8 x10 framed photo of him. I loved the picture, but what brought tears to my eyes was all the work and money involved to get that gift put together. He had taken the photo card out of the camera and rode his bike to Walgreens down the street. He paid to have the photo enlarged and printed, as well as for the frame. He used his own money. Then, he came home and got the photo in the frame before wrapping it all up. He had it all done prior to me coming home so that I could be surprised. Wow! His thoughtfulness gave me the chills. This is typical for the Ethan I know. He loves to be independent and can figure out how to complete a task. He also loves to do nice things for people. It is a memory and a gift that I will forever treasure.

Because Seroquel was working so well, we decided to take Ethan's dose of Seroquel all the way up to the maximum dose of 800mg a day. This way we would be able to find the best dose for him and see if maybe this medicine could be the only one he would need. As we did that, he started to become more agitated and impulsive. We realized that it was better at the lower dosage of 500mg total so we lowered it back down. Things were really so much better, but I still had some concerns. He would get irritated if triggered, he was still having a lot of anxiety issues, and his tolerance level was fairly low. Since all of his symptoms were not taken care of with Seroquel, Dr. Roy decided to add another medication to it. He added Neurontin because we can increase the dose fast in order to know what results we get. He also felt that it might help with his anxiety. It didn't take long for us to know that it was not going to work for him. It also activated him like many of the medicines before.

In January at the beginning of the second semester, Ethan went back to school on a part time basis. Our household made good use of the additional income, as I went back to work part time as well. Mr. Zoelle welcomed both of us back part time and it allowed us to see how things would go. Since Ethan was feeling better about everything, he was anxious to get back to a more normal setting and see all of his friends again. We started him off at just a couple of hours each day and then increased his hours according to his capabilities and needs. He ended the year attending most of his core classes going from 10:15 till 3:00 each day. The reason he needed the late start was because it is very difficult to wake him up. He sleeps approximately 11 to 12 hours a night. Trying to get him up and at school each day by 8:00am would have been too hard and stressful. Luckily, Mr. Zoelle was willing to try something new and it sure paid off for us. Another mood stabilizer called Lamictal was added to his Seroquel during that semester. It seemed to help even things out for him and he was able to have a fairly positive school experience the second half of seventh grade. I never felt that he was completely accepted back by the other students, but I don't believe anyone was mean to him either. It may have been just an awkward situation all the way around. As we were changing and moving around his morning Seroquel dose, we did notice some unwanted issues with him and a few girls start to bloom. It let me know that he needed the morning Seroquel and the teachers helped keep a watchful eye so as nothing else would continue. We hope positive developments will continue through his eighth grade year as well. He would like to graduate eighth grade from there with his friends and I don't blame him. St. Matthew has certainly been an intricate part of our lives for the past ten years and I feel strongly that it was not an accident.

Pieces to the Puzzle

- Likes to be off on his bike – freedom to roam
- Narrow focus
- Doesn't see options well
- Stomach troubles at times
- Low threshold of embarrassment
- Excessive worry about what others think
- Over reacts emotionally
- Forgetful
- Negativity
- Happier
- Rages are less frequent and shorter lasting
- Sleeps better
- More pleasant
- More helpful around the house

7th Grade Home School...

Since the medicine wasn't helping yet, my mom decided that I should be home schooled. My friends wondered why I was staying home and my mom said to blame it on her. So, I did. I liked the idea and was happy to not be going back to school. I could sleep in, I didn't have to wear a uniform, and the work would be easier. I also got to go to a construction site near my house and watch them work. If I were in school, I wouldn't have been able to do much of that.

Some of my favorite things that we did for school were going to Discovery Cove and building a cat condo. Discovery Cove was amazing and I would love to go back. I got to swim with a dolphin and snorkel with a lot of other sea creatures. I liked petting the sting rays too. I have wanted to buy or build a cat condo for a long time. My mom finally said we were going to build it for school. I was happy. It took a long time and it was kind of hard.

There are some things I don't like about home schooling too. I don't get to see my friends very much and I couldn't play school soccer. Instead I joined a new soccer team called the Strikers. This team is harder and the season is longer, but I'm glad I joined so I could still play.

After trying Trileptal for several months and it not working, I was switched to Seroquel. It was different right away. I felt happier. I had to keep taking more of it so Dr. Roy could decide what the right amount was for me. It makes me sleepy and I have gained a little weight. I hate that I have gained weight and hope it goes away. I also think I lost some of my memory while I have been taking it. It has been hard trying to write this book because I have had a hard time remembering everything.

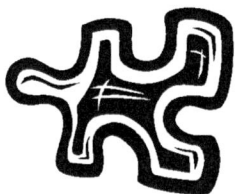

Future Plans...

I realize that there is a long road ahead of us. As much as I want to live in the moment and enjoy the present, I also need to plan for the future. I now realize how important routine and daily life is for Ethan. We have always been pretty conservative and consistent, but I will now plan on being more intentional about our schedule and avoid over scheduling. I will try to stay on top of medications, side effects, and his general good health. My diligence in knowing what is going on in his life will be crucial to preventing and/or stopping behaviors that could be dangerous for him. In order to do that, our relationship has to stay strong. It will mean developing into a different kind of parent than what I had become. I will pick my battles very carefully and make sure he knows how much I love him. I will need to continue to learn as much as I can and help to educate him so that he has a clear understanding of himself with this disorder. I will need to get together a plan for emergencies in case one should arise. For instance, I will need to understand what his insurance will cover for treatment and where treatment centers are located. Jim and I will need to prioritize our finances and somehow put money aside in case we need to go through more of these kinds of times.

Getting through middle school will be our first goal. Hopefully, we will be able to make things work at St. Matthew because of the understanding and flexibility we will find there. This will give me approximately one year to try to keep our life running smoothly and continue to learn how to best meet Ethan's needs. High school is really what I am most concerned about right now.

At this point, I have been unable to find a school in our area that would best serve his needs. The public school system is a "cookie cutter" approach with the main focus on FCAT scores. The school discipline plans are based on zero tolerance rules given the current climate of violence in our society. The schools are very populated and these conditions lead me to believe that they would not provide the kind of environment Ethan would need. A student who qualifies for exceptional student education (ESE) can be placed in special classes or even special schools, but in many cases a student needs to be failing or in severe trouble for that to happen. Even though Ethan might qualify for ESE services based on medical proof, I don't think it would be in his best interest to be educated with that group of students. In theory, the programs seem as though they are set up to help students, however, I have witnessed first hand how local public schools and/or programs designed to help students like Ethan can be degrading and lead to a feeling of being a failure for the student. Many times the students can actually learn worse behavior by connecting with other students who have behavioral problems. I feel certain that it would devastate Ethan if he were to be thought of as an ESE student or placed in a special needs classroom because he does not identify himself as being that type of student or person.

There are a few private schools that cater to special needs, but they are mainly for students with learning disabilities and those who are below grade level. Those aren't right for him either. I did have an administrator of one of those schools validate that for me as well. My hope is that he may be able to take some of his courses online with the Florida Virtual School and attend some classes on a public high school campus (dual enrollment). This way he is not at school too long during the day, but is getting all of his course work completed while not appearing to be that out of the ordinary to anyone. It would also mean that he would not have to get up as early in the morning which is a huge issue for him. I could drive him to and from school which would eliminate additional problems with peers. I plan on approaching the school system and administrators next school year with this idea to see if it can work.

If I dare to dream, I would like to see a school that took a more individualized route. It would be an alternative to a traditional public school, but not because the students failed prior to coming there. Dr. Levine's Schools Attuned program could come in to play for helping students with learning differences, but basically it would be set up to deal with individuals rather than the masses. Students could progress at different paces with different types of curriculum. The use of virtual schools and distance learning might be helpful. The typical school schedule may not even be necessary. Accommodations could be made to help with necessities. The school should be large enough so that it feels like a normal school, but small enough for the mission to remain manageable. Standardized test scores would be used to determine academic needs and levels of the individual students as opposed to being used to grade and compensate the school itself. The presentation of the content makes a huge difference in whether or not students become interested in the subject matter. Finding innovative and creative ways to reach students would be very important. That is one reason why the most important aspect of the school would be the staff. A good staff can accomplish almost anything and a good staff should be treated so well that they never want to leave. Each and every member of the staff in that school would have the desire to work with all kinds of students. They would be excited about the prospect of making a different kind of school. They would want to be a lifelong learner. The training that the administration and staff receive is critical. It would be heavy in the initial start up phase and continue each year. The plan being that the turnover rate would be small and the staff would just increase in their knowledge, skills, ideas, and satisfaction over the years. It would be a school where thinking outside of the box in order to meet the needs of their students is expected. Students would feel welcome there and understood. It would be a place where students are expected to excel and are given the tools needed to do so. The ability level of the students would vary, but it may be a good idea to concentrate on average to gifted IQs since there are already programs in place for lower IQs and learning disabilities. The community would support that school and partner up with it knowing that it could truly be making a difference in society. It would be those students who might have easily dropped out of another school, self medicated themselves with drugs and alcohol, or turned to a life a crime because they felt lost, bored, and misunderstood. Instead, that kind of school would be giving them the opportunity to be successful academically as well as personally and those same students could easily become business, artistic, or community leaders.

I would love to have a place like that for Ethan. I would even help to start a school like that if I had the chance. It is a huge undertaking and I don't know where to begin or who else to speak with about the idea. I will continue to voice my opinion though, in hopes that I finally find the appropriate forum for its discussion.

Another dream I have for our community is a brain center. I notice heart and other medical centers exists so why not a brain center. It could be called Brain Works and under this one umbrella could be many facets and services. I would love for us to have a SPECT scan available along with other types of scans. Neurologist, psychiatrist, and psychologist could all work together as a team on many clients. The NAMI office and other mental health organizations could be based in the center as well. Counseling and alternative treatment options could be found in this same center. I would also like to include educational areas and a resource library. There could even be residential and/or part time programs available to the community.

As a matter of fact, many great things have been born from adversity. I hope that can happen for us as well. I hope to use what I have learned and my thirst for answers to evoke positive change in some fashion. Some of my other ideas for myself include teaching a university class in the college of education that includes neurological disorders and individual differences in learners, presenting information to existing school teaching staffs, consulting with other parents in similar situations, and aligning myself with an organization designed to promote public awareness and increase funds for research. I think it is extremely important to pass on current research and real people's experiences in order to inform the public on what "mental illness" really is. Everyone needs to understand that it is some form of a brain disorder and it is no one's fault when a person has it. We have learned a lot about most of our body's organs and there is much sympathy towards people with medical conditions. The same needs to happen for brain disorders. I feel confident that we can understand the brain better than we do now and that there will be great treatment options in the future. However, I worry that the stigma associated with people who have these various brain disorders will ruin the pace and progression of its understanding and cure. I hope to be able to change people's perspective on it for our sake as well as for others who follow us.

The Future...

Right now, I am planning on finishing 7th grade at St. Matthew, but going part time. Then I will probably go there for 8th grade and graduate from that school. I want to go to a particular public high school. I want to go there because my step brother goes there. I don't know what college I will go to or what I will study. I am interested in construction and driving trucks (like semis).

I know that I might have to take medicine for the rest of my life. I hope one day they have a cure for bipolar so that I won't have to take medicine and I can just be normal with out it. I don't want surgery, but I would do it if it would fix my brain. Sometimes I worry that I won't be able to do everything that I need to as an adult. I know that drugs and alcohol are bad for everyone, but especially someone like me. I hope I don't use them.

I think everyone is perfect in heaven and I look forward to being perfect one day.

What I have learned about Early-Onset Bipolar Disorder…

I have learned so much about early-onset bipolar disorder through a variety of sources. I believe that it is very important to be well informed and knowledgeable about any condition affecting your life or the life of a loved one.

It is important to know that early-onset bipolar disorder differs from bipolar in adults. Children's bodies are still developing and this disorder may present itself differently in a child than it does in an adult. Children may not have the same cycling patterns associated with adult bipolar disorder. In a child, it may present itself as an overall moodiness or irritability for an example.

Most importantly, I learned that any bipolar disorder is a brain disorder and is inherited approximately 98% of the time. This enlightenment is what allowed me to see the behavior of my son differently. I no longer question his motives or feel disappointed with his lack of self control. I view things such as those as symptoms of a disorder much the same way that diabetes has symptoms. Most brain functions have to do with genetic, electrical responses, and neurotransmitter chemicals. When something is off, even by a little bit, it can produce a domino effect of problems. This disorder is invisible to the naked eye, just like diabetes, so we have to be able to recognize certain behaviors as symptoms instead of treating them as poor choices.

I have also learned that there are a lot more of these children out there than I ever felt was possible. I have met many parents who are concerned about their child's emotional stability, many of which have already been diagnosed with bipolar. In the past, I felt alone and misunderstood. Through finding others in this situation in my community as well as in support groups, I have felt connected and validated in my feelings and efforts. It is amazing how some parts of everyone's stories are so similar. Children who have never met before are exhibiting the same behaviors that parents thought were just individual quirks. With that being said, it is also true that bipolar can present itself differently in each individual and have varying degrees of severity so it is difficult for a person to make that diagnosis.

I have learned that it is very likely for children to display ADHD type behaviors as a first sign of bipolar. It is very common for children to be misdiagnosed with ADHD and placed on inappropriate medications. There are cases, however, where some children have co-occurring disorders of bipolar and ADHD. Learning the signs and symptoms of bipolar have come through our own experiences, books I have read, and listening to other people's stories. There are many possible symptoms but I have narrowed down the list to a few that really stand out to me. Constant irritability and low tolerance level is something I associate with early-onset bipolar. I also associate things like rages, inflexibility, explosiveness, sleep problems, social problems, excessive crying, and anxiety with it as well. Many children with bipolar speak of death and are unhappy with their lives. The biggest red flag for me is when these symptoms occur with children that should otherwise be happy, positive, and well-behaved. When there is a clear difference between what the family life style and parenting is and the behaviors the child is exhibiting, it makes me want to take a closer look at the child's brain functioning.

Thank goodness I have been able to learn about treatment plans for the disorder and lifestyle changes that can help as well. I believe treatment is the key to stability, which is the key to a positive lifestyle. I have learned some simple things that help in our household. If I can remain calm and keep my reactions to a minimum, it helps Ethan remain calm. He is able to pick up on slight changes in my tone or mood and he finds it very discomforting. I also found that it is helpful to give him warnings or set times of when to expect a change. I do not expect all the things of him that I once did because the pressure and stress of trying to keep up with everything upsets him. He needs a good amount of sleep in a consistent manner. I have allowed him to drop from some extra curricular activities in order to have a simpler schedule. Aside from these lifestyle changes, medication and/or supplements are a priority in treatment. Finding the correct medication and correct dosage can help immensely because stability can be achieved. Once at that point, therapy, education, and even behavior modification can all work more effectively.

Unfortunately, I have learned that most people know very little about brain disorders like bipolar, even the professionals. I believe that we are on the brink of unlocking the secrets of the brain and gaining a better understanding of how to help people with these disorders. Universities and professionals in their fields presently need to become better informed and catch up to what the research is showing us. Parents need answers and the professionals involved need to be able to provide them. I have learned that I can not be ashamed of his medical condition. If I were to send that message to him, it could undermine his treatment and feelings about what he can achieve. There is a stigma in our society associated with "mental illness" that needs to be done away with. The only way I know to do that is to educate people with the truths. I know my child does not have a weak character. I know that I have done a fine job of parenting. I know that if he could do better, he would. People who don't understand these things tend to deny the possibility of a biophysical problem. They disconnect from those diagnosed with disorders like bipolar. They tend to put blame anywhere but where it belongs and it destroys relationships. I have learned that if my son had cancer or needed an organ transplant the support from family, friends, and strangers would be significant and visible. Having bipolar disorder means that it is hard to share our situation with others. It also means that people don't understand nor know what to say. There is very little verbal, moral, or financial support from anyone. I know that everyone's support is needed, not only by my family but by all people whose lives have been affected by bipolar disorder.

What I have learned about Bipolar Disorder....

Until someone told me I had bipolar, I had never even heard of it. I have learned that it is a brain disorder and it can affect your moods. Before taking medicine I was very mad all of the time and was mad for no reason at all. I hated my life. I have learned that taking the right medicine has helped in many ways. Now I am happier and in a good mood most of the time. Life is a lot better. I have learned that having bipolar is not anyone's fault.

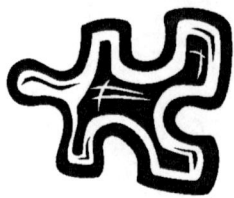

Final Thoughts....

Obviously, no one can say what will happen tomorrow, next year, five years, or thirty years from now. For us, it is just more uncertain. Even though I don't know our future, I have learned from looking back on my past that God knows our future. In fact, he has a plan for each of us and knowing that helps me to see hope in the future. I can say that I plan to continue everything possible to support and encourage Ethan's positive health and growth. My prayers will not cease and my love for him will be forever unconditional. I will expect our life to be anything but boring and mundane.

Ultimately, it will become his journey to continue as he grows into an adult. Having him gain acceptance and understanding of this disorder will help him to feel proud of himself as opposed to being ashamed of his bipolar condition. As this journey continues to be our everyday life, I also believe that our story is preparation and inspiration for somebody else, maybe you.

I plan to create a website where I can share more information with others. I also want to continue sharing what is going on in our life. If you are interested in reading more, please visit www.thebrainpiece.com.

Random Thoughts about Me...

I notice stuff that people usually don't.

I can think and see in a different perspective than my own. Say I am at a stop light and there is a car directly across from me, I can put myself in their perspective and I can see what he sees looking at my mom's car. It happens anytime I want it to.

I like music playing while I am doing whatever, working to just hanging out.

I hate reading but I love soccer.

I have to do stuff like 25 times and then I can stop. There is a number in my head even before I do it.

I hate most meat. I love sweets.

I am afraid of the outside darkness when I am by myself.

I worry about what people think about me.

I like laughing.

I don't like to be told "no".

I have a lot of bad dreams.

I wish I could own a front loader, had millions of dollars, and that my mom and my dad were still married.

I like having friends.

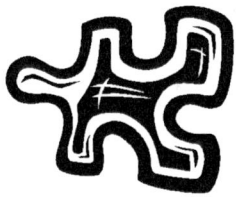

Frequently asked Questions...

Q: **Children are often stubborn and irritable. How do I know the difference between what is normal and what is abnormal?**

A: I believe this has to be considered on an individual basis. I am not a medical doctor and would never try to provide someone with a diagnosis. However, I have spent the past twenty years around children and have gone through the process of unlocking the mystery with my own son. For me, I felt that his behaviors were excessive and beyond the range of normal. I felt that he often over reacted and wasn't realistic about some things. I also knew how much effort and time I had put into parenting him in a consistent loving manner and was able to see that I wasn't getting the positive results that I felt we should have seen. The bottom line was that I felt in my gut that something was not right. I often let people's opinions and comments (like "boys will be boys" and "he just likes to push your buttons") influence my gut feelings, but in the end I needed to act on those motherly instincts.

If a teacher(s) talks to you about learning or behavioral problems, you should take note. They spend a lot of time around children in the same age group as your child and should be able to recognize many abnormalities. They may not be able to explain the reasons for it though, so that is where you would come in with your experiences, family history, and observations.

Q: What did you do about the rest of your family while you were working with Ethan?

> A: Having a blended family has its own set of issues, but one way that it was helpful was that my husband had been very involved in his boys' lives and had a lot going on with them as I was working on things with Ethan. We do not have any children together so the divide and conquer method works fairly well when we need it. About half of the time, Ethan is the only child in our home which may also help in keeping things calm and simple. My husband has been supportive through everything, even when he really didn't have a good understanding of early- onset bipolar disorder. We have been honest with family members and at the same time try to keep our normal family routines and traditions consistent.

Q: What did you do for yourself to help you make it through the tough times?

> A: My self help program consists of keeping my faith, acquiring knowledge on the subject, maintaining family and friends relationships, staying involved with the things that interest me, joining a support group, and beginning to advocate for my child. I have tried to exercise more regularly and eat more healthily, but I haven't been as successful as I should be yet. A few other tips I can offer are to think positively, communicate well with others, think about the serenity prayer, and utilize team work.

Q: Can you tell us more about Ethan's father and how he is doing?

> A: I wish I understood bipolar 10 years ago when he was diagnosed with it the way I understand it today and maybe I would have been able to have helped him more. Unfortunately, he has gone untreated all these years. One bad decision or circumstance has led to another in his life. He has always maintained his relationship with Ethan, but has not been able to provide for him emotionally or financially on

any consistent basis. Currently, we are encouraging him to try medication and he seems more willing to accept his diagnosis and possibly give treatment a try. That would be great for Ethan in more ways than one.

Q: I think there may be something wrong with my child's brain. What should I do?

A: There are a few key things that I would suggest you do. First, I would see what your area has to offer for mental health in the way of doctors, resources, educational programs, etc. Then you will want to find a medical doctor and/or a psychiatrist who really understands brain disorders. Before you go to the first appointment I suggest that you explore your child's family history. Write down for the doctor anyone who has had difficulty with things like school work, depression, addictions, food disorders, OCD, and suicide attempts and/or completions. Those are very important because of the strong connection with brain disorders and heredity. I would also start learning all that you can about the various disorders and medications. That way, when you see a professional you will know the things to discuss with him and understand what he has to say about the possibilities. You can work together as a team to help your child. I encourage people to explore the idea of having a SPECT scan done as well. If you have the resources and desire to go that route, I don't think you'll be disappointed.

Q: My child is diagnosed with ADHD. How do I know if it is the right diagnosis or not?

A: I do believe that many children really do have ADHD, but I also believe that misdiagnoses happen too. Please remember that I am not a doctor, nor do I have any medical training. I am not sure how you can be absolutely sure of the diagnosis, but there are a few things you can do to help discover the answer. One of things would be to have a SPECT scan done. I feel that technology similar to this is used for almost every other part of the body, why wouldn't we use it for our brains too? As long as you have competent people reading the scans and advising your doctor, I feel that it is great tool. It would also be important to take a look at how your child reacts to the medication they are prescribed. If it is a stimulant and it appears to make them more irritable, sad, angry, etc., that could be a sign that it is the wrong diagnosis and/or wrong medication. If you're not sure, try taking them off the medication (under a doctor's care, of course) and see what changes occur. Like I said earlier, I have seen children make great gains and really benefit from ADHD medication, when it was right for them. You may have to have opinions from multiple doctors in order to find one that is willing to really investigate your concerns. The other thing you can do is to learn as much as you can and trust your instincts.

Q: What should I say to the teacher/school about my child's illness?

A: It is important that the school and teacher(s) know about any testing results and diagnosis with your child. They will not be able to meet the needs of the child if they don't know what they are. With that said, most educators lack knowledge about the problem and how to help with the problem. Keep in mind that the mental illness stigma is also alive and well in the educational field. You can help educate them by providing them with resources on bipolar disorder and the symptoms associated with it. You should share your concerns and ideas. If your child is part of exceptional student education (ESE) please refer to web sites such as www.starfishadvocacy.org and www.wrightslaw.com for more advice.

Q: What can be done to help with mental health awareness and support?

A: A lot! Education seems to be a huge factor in getting people to have a different perspective on the subject. Educate yourself and then continue to educate others. I think it is important for people working in the political arena, medical profession, insurance industry, educational profession, and the mental health profession to all be active in gaining an up-to-date view on the issues and pursue ways to make all aspects better for our society. Money for research is another way that people can help. It takes a lot of money and time to develop medications, tools, programs, hospitals, etc. that are needed for mental health improvement. Get involved however works best for you and your family, but get involved.

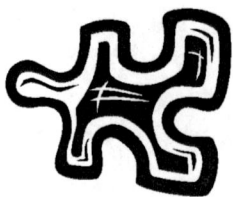

Resources We Depend on...

Dr. Omar Rieche- www.riechemd.com Dr. Rieche is Ethan's psychiatrist locally. He has worked very well with me in trying to solve the mystery and then appropriately treat the problem. There are not enough good children's psychiatrists around, so I know that his schedule is always quite full. Hopefully, there will be more like him to provide what is necessary for our children.

Brain Matters, Inc. -www.brainmattersinc.com This is where Ethan had his SPECT scan done. I was very happy with the service they provided and the friendliness of the staff. The findings from the scan have helped me to identify and understand the problems. They have also helped Dr. Rieche with the treatment. They have continued to provide information and support over the past year.

Dr. Daniel Amen- www.amenclinics.com His clinics also provide SPECT scans to their patients. His website has a lot of good information on it. He has written many books that I highly recommend and they are all on his site. He has a lot of knowledge about supplements as well as medications to use for treatments. I often am referring to one of his books where Ethan's treatment is concerned.

The Bipolar Child- www.bipolarchild.com This book was written by Demitri and Janice Papolos originally in 2000. It has paved the way for many authors since then to share information on this topic. It is recognized for being an excellent source of information on early-onset bipolar disorder. I read it when I first suspected bipolar and continue to go back through its pages from time to time.

Child and Adolescent Bipolar Foundation- www.bpkids.org This a great website and a wealth of information for you. The greatest benefit that I have received from the site is the online support group that I have been part of for the past year. There is compassion, support, help, and information at the touch of your keyboard.

NAMI- www.nami.org NAMI (National Alliance on Mental Illness) is a voice for mental illness in this country. The organization has educational and support programs for all involved. They also work to help change and pass laws in favor of helping those with mental illness. They also have resources that can be beneficial. I have taken the Family to Family course and am continuing to help our county affiliate in whatever way that I can.

ISBN 142512773-8